ASSASSIN'S CREED®
BLOODSTONE

BOOK 2

< **WRITER** >
< GUILLAUME DORISON >

<**ARTIST**>
< ENNIO BUFI >

< **COLORIST** >
< ANDREA MELONI >

< TRANSLATION >
< MARC BOURBON-CROOK >

< LETTERING >
< JONATHAN STEVENSON >

THE ASSASSIN'S CREED LIBRARY

ASSASSIN'S CREED VOLUME 1: **TRIAL BY FIRE**
ASSASSIN'S CREED VOLUME 2: **SETTING SUN**
ASSASSIN'S CREED VOLUME 3: **HOMECOMING**
ASSASSIN'S CREED TEMPLARS VOLUME 1: **BLACK CROSS**
ASSASSIN'S CREED TEMPLARS VOLUME 2: **CROSS OF WAR**
ASSASSIN'S CREED UPRISING VOLUME 1: **COMMON GROUND**
ASSASSIN'S CREED UPRISING VOLUME 2: **INFLECTION POINT**
ASSASSIN'S CREED UPRISING VOLUME 3: **FINALE**
ASSASSIN'S CREED: **REFLECTIONS**
ASSASSIN'S CREED: **LAST DESCENDANTS – LOCUS**
ASSASSIN'S CREED: **AWAKENING VOLUME 1**
ASSASSIN'S CREED: **AWAKENING VOLUME 2**
ASSASSIN'S CREED: **ORIGINS**
ASSASSIN'S CREED: **CONSPIRACIES**
ASSASSIN'S CREED: **THE FALL & THE CHAIN**
ASSASSIN'S CREED: **BLOODSTONE BOOK 1**
ASSASSIN'S CREED: **BLOODSTONE BOOK 2**

TITAN COMICS

EDITOR TOLLY MAGGS
SENIOR DESIGNER ANDREW LEUNG
SENIOR CREATIVE EDITOR DAVID LEACH
MANAGING EDITOR MARTIN EDEN
PRODUCTION CONTROLLER CATERINA FALQUI
SENIOR PRODUCTION CONTROLLER JACKIE FLOOK
ART DIRECTOR OZ BROWNE
SALES & CIRCULATION MANAGER STEVE TOTHILL
PUBLICIST IMOGEN HARRIS
DIRECT MARKETING ASSISTANT GEORGE WICKENDEN
MARKETING MANAGER RICKY CLAYDON
HEAD OF RIGHTS JENNY BOYCE
EDITORIAL DIRECTOR DUNCAN BAIZLEY
OPERATIONS DIRECTOR LEIGH BAULCH
EXECUTIVE DIRECTOR VIVIAN CHEUNG
PUBLISHER NICK LANDAU

9781787734593

A CIP catalogue record for this title is available from the British Library

First edition: November 2020
10 9 8 7 6 5 4 3 2 1
Printed in China.

WWW.TITAN-COMICS.COM
Follow us on Twitter @ComicsTitan
Visit us at facebook.com/comicstitan

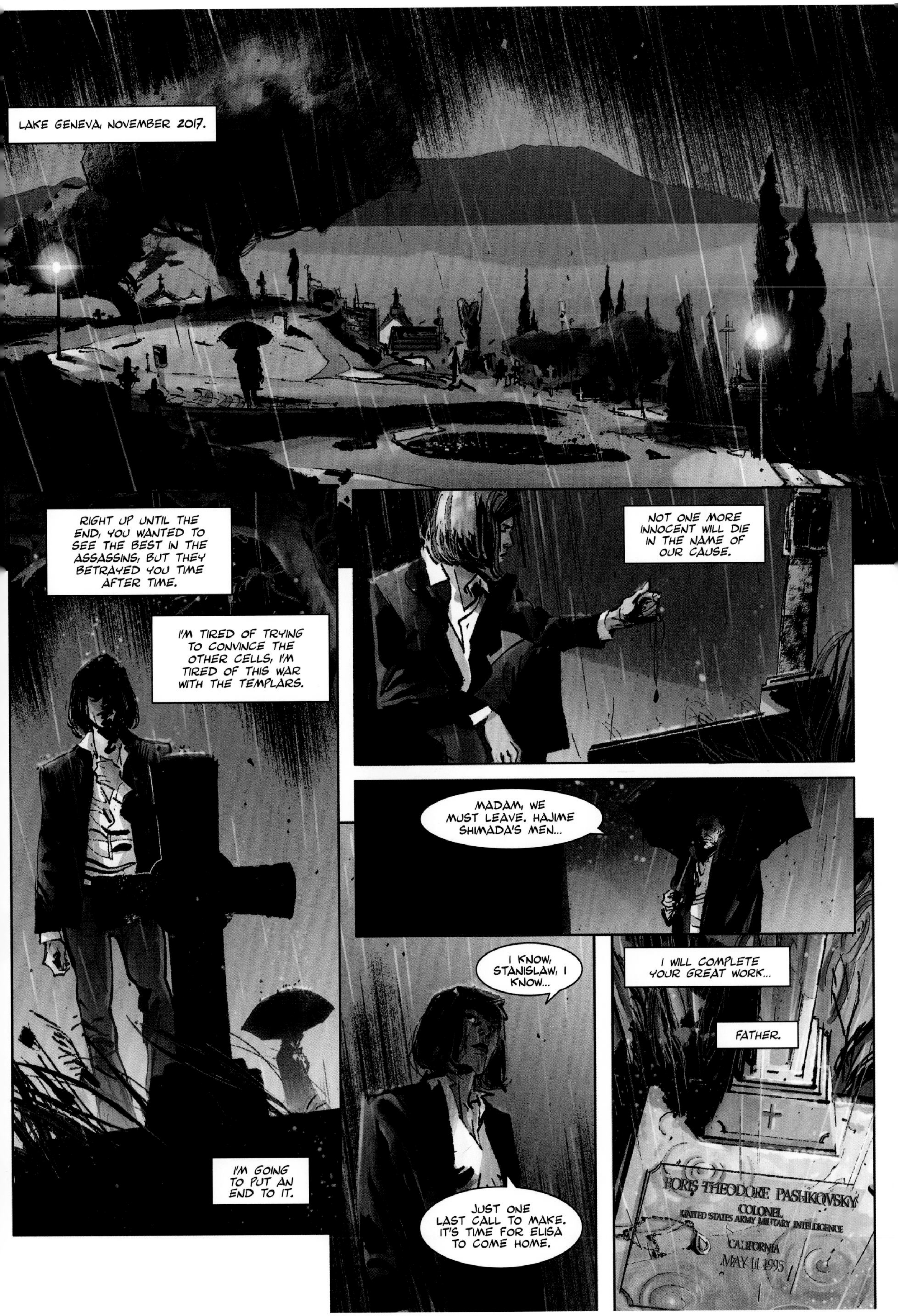
LAKE GENEVA, NOVEMBER 2017.
RIGHT UP UNTIL THE END, YOU WANTED TO SEE THE BEST IN THE ASSASSINS, BUT THEY BETRAYED YOU TIME AFTER TIME.
I'M TIRED OF TRYING TO CONVINCE THE OTHER CELLS, I'M TIRED OF THIS WAR WITH THE TEMPLARS.
I'M GOING TO PUT AN END TO IT.
NOT ONE MORE INNOCENT WILL DIE IN THE NAME OF OUR CAUSE.
MADAM, WE MUST LEAVE. HAJIME SHIMADA'S MEN...
I KNOW, STANISLAW, I KNOW...
JUST ONE LAST CALL TO MAKE. IT'S TIME FOR ELISA TO COME HOME.
I WILL COMPLETE YOUR GREAT WORK...
FATHER.
BORIS THEODORE PASHKOVSKY
COLONEL
UNITED STATES ARMY MILITARY INTELLIGENCE
CALIFORNIA
MAY 11 1995

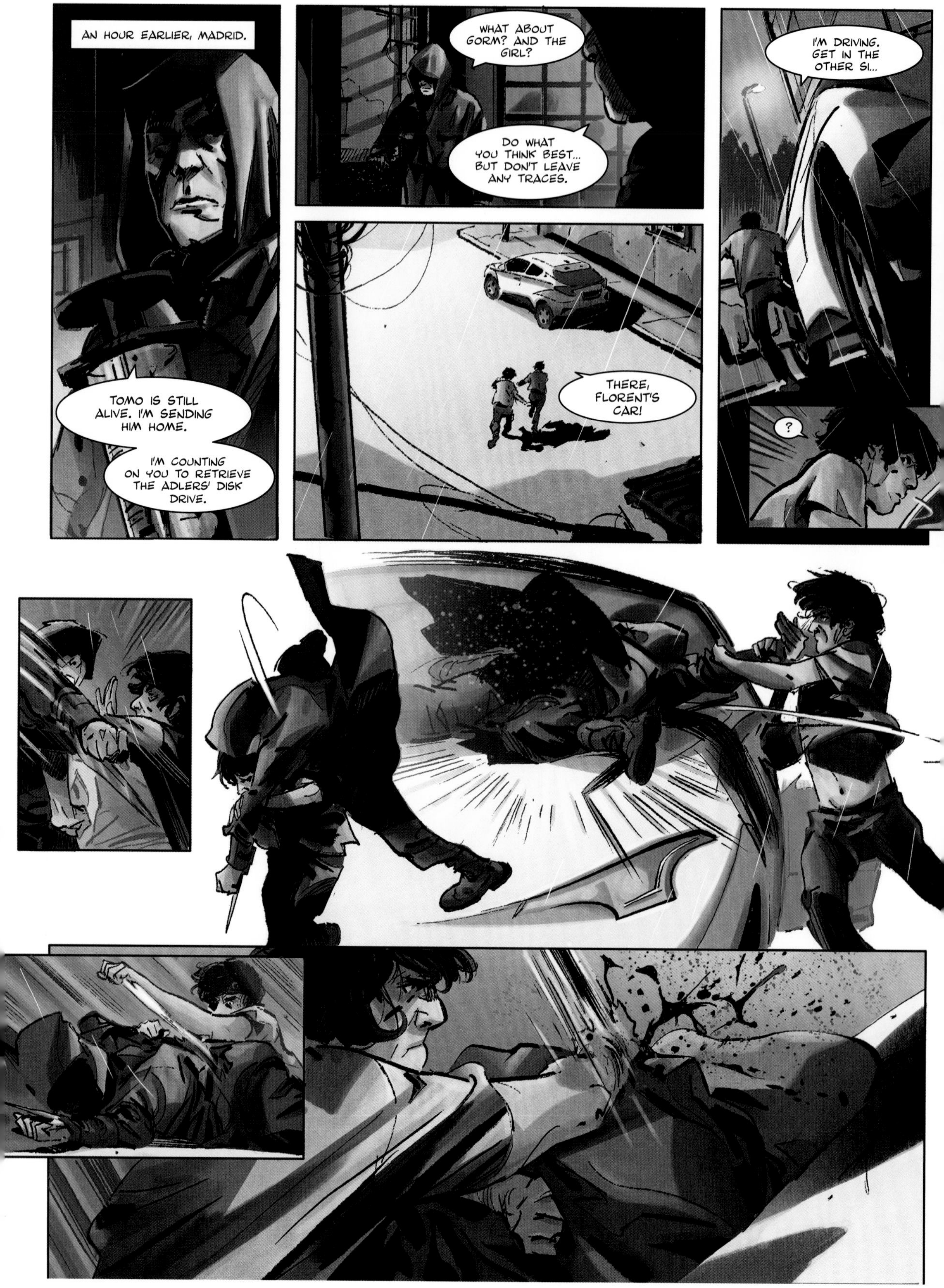
AN HOUR EARLIER, MADRID.
TOMO IS STILL ALIVE. I'M SENDING HIM HOME.
I'M COUNTING ON YOU TO RETRIEVE THE ADLERS' DISK DRIVE.
WHAT ABOUT GORM? AND THE GIRL?
DO WHAT YOU THINK BEST... BUT DON'T LEAVE ANY TRACES.
THERE, FLORENT'S CAR!
I'M DRIVING. GET IN THE OTHER SI...
?

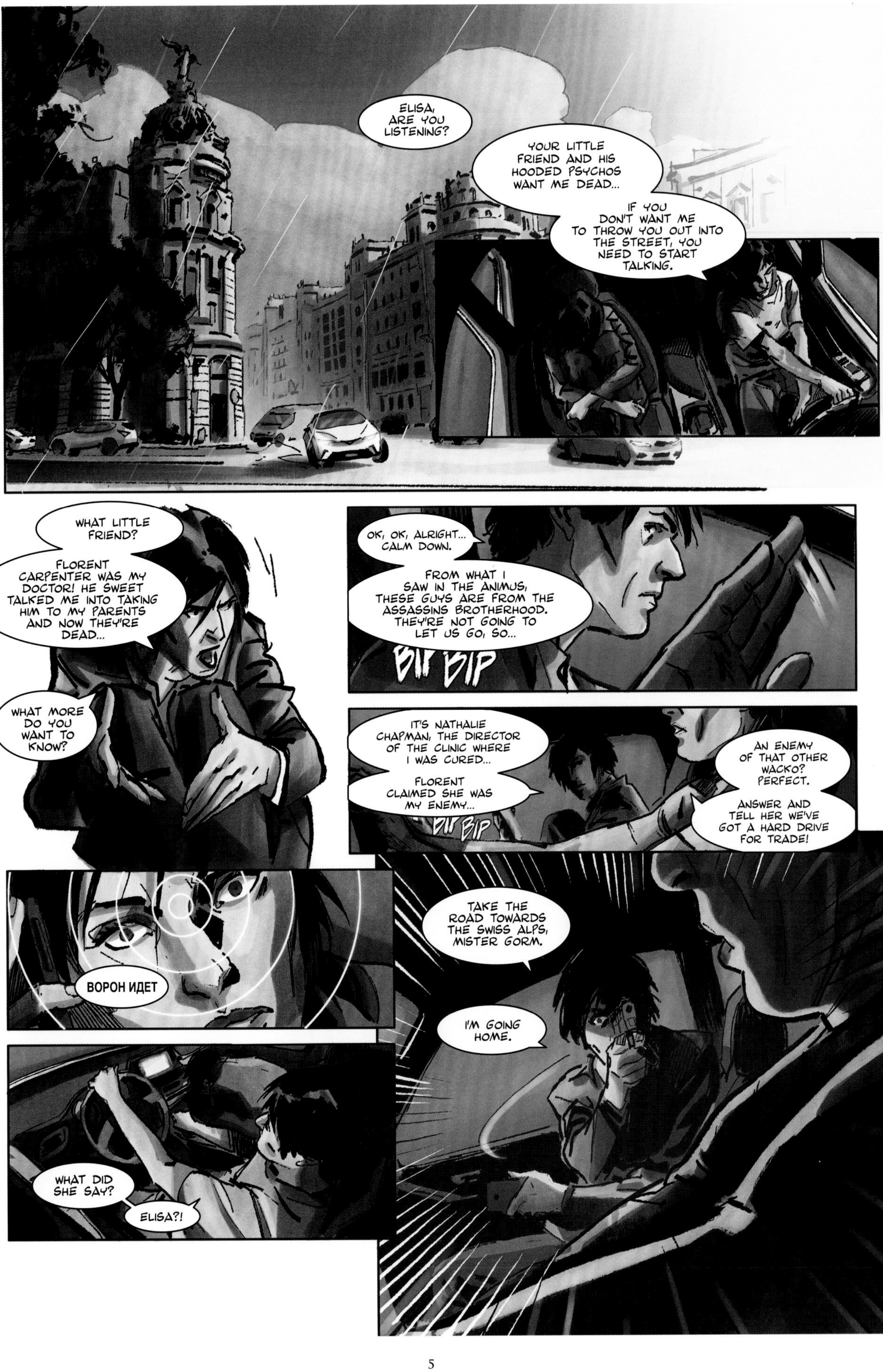
ELISA, ARE YOU LISTENING?
YOUR LITTLE FRIEND AND HIS HOODED PSYCHOS WANT ME DEAD...
IF YOU DON'T WANT ME TO THROW YOU OUT INTO THE STREET, YOU NEED TO START TALKING.
WHAT LITTLE FRIEND?
FLORENT CARPENTER WAS MY DOCTOR! HE SWEET TALKED ME INTO TAKING HIM TO MY PARENTS AND NOW THEY'RE DEAD...
WHAT MORE DO YOU WANT TO KNOW?
OK, OK, ALRIGHT... CALM DOWN.
FROM WHAT I SAW IN THE ANIMUS, THESE GUYS ARE FROM THE ASSASSINS BROTHERHOOD. THEY'RE NOT GOING TO LET US GO, SO...
BIP BIP
IT'S NATHALIE CHAPMAN, THE DIRECTOR OF THE CLINIC WHERE I WAS CURED...
FLORENT CLAIMED SHE WAS MY ENEMY...
BIP BIP
AN ENEMY OF THAT OTHER WACKO? PERFECT.
ANSWER AND TELL HER WE'VE GOT A HARD DRIVE FOR TRADE!
ВОРОН ИДЕТ
WHAT DID SHE SAY?
ELISA?!
TAKE THE ROAD TOWARDS THE SWISS ALPS, MISTER GORM.
I'M GOING HOME.

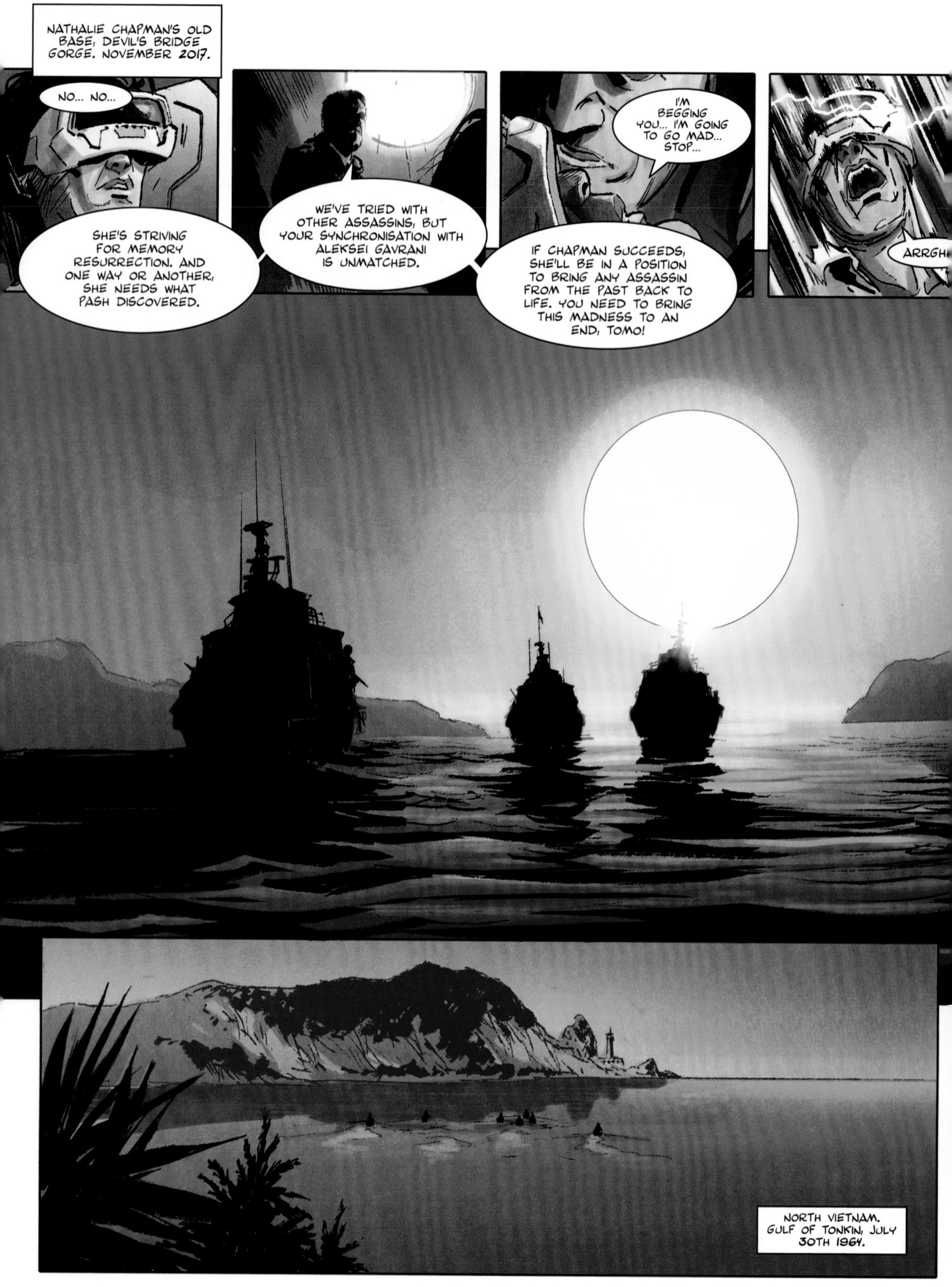
NATHALIE CHAPMAN'S OLD BASE, DEVIL'S BRIDGE GORGE. NOVEMBER 2017.
NO... NO...
SHE'S STRIVING FOR MEMORY RESURRECTION. AND ONE WAY OR ANOTHER, SHE NEEDS WHAT PASH DISCOVERED.
WE'VE TRIED WITH OTHER ASSASSINS, BUT YOUR SYNCHRONISATION WITH ALEKSEI GAVRANI IS UNMATCHED.
I'M BEGGING YOU... I'M GOING TO GO MAD... STOP...
IF CHAPMAN SUCCEEDS, SHE'LL BE IN A POSITION TO BRING ANY ASSASSIN FROM THE PAST BACK TO LIFE. YOU NEED TO BRING THIS MADNESS TO AN END, TOMO!
ARRGH
NORTH VIETNAM. GULF OF TONKIN, JULY 30TH 1964.

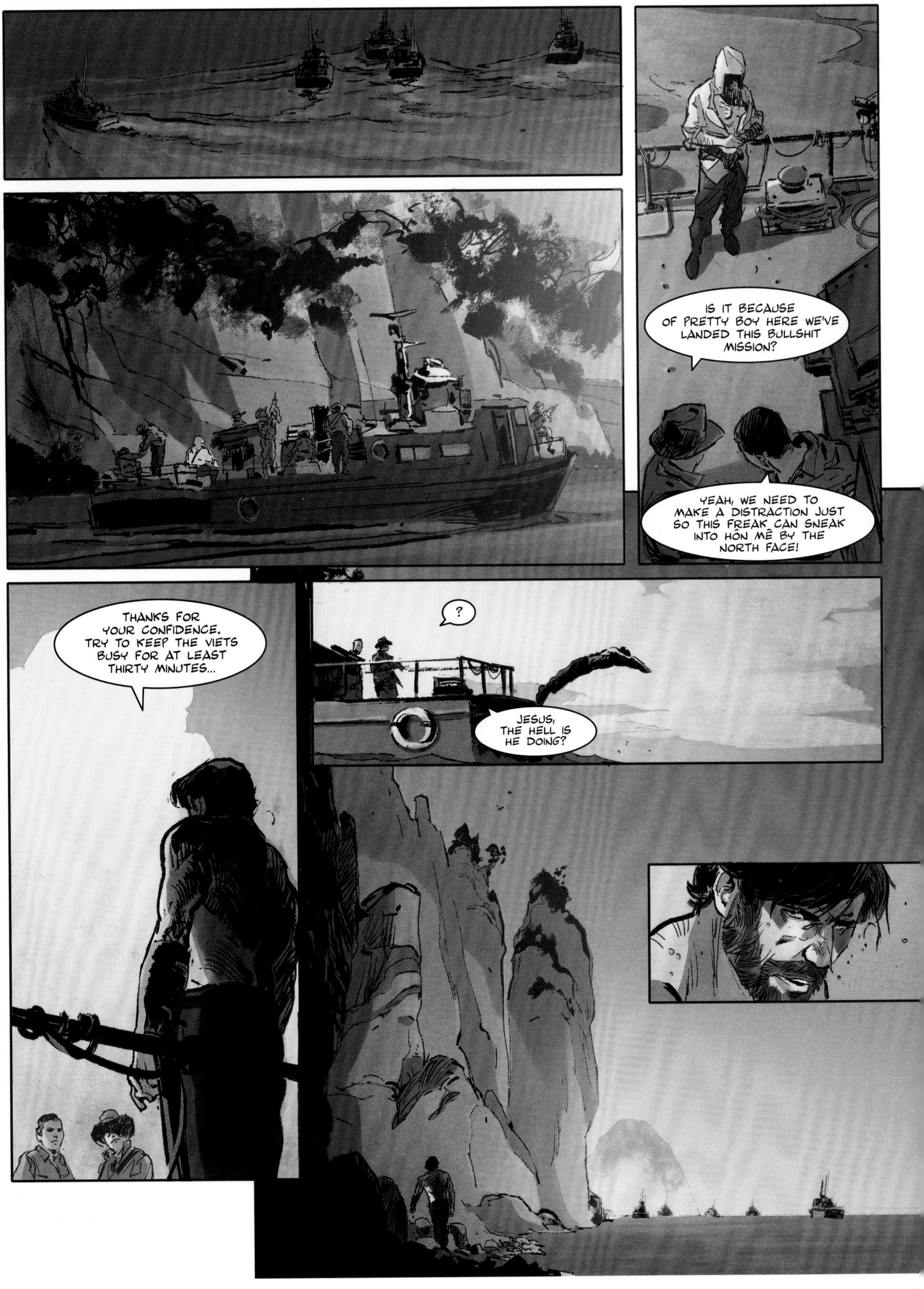
IS IT BECAUSE OF PRETTY BOY HERE WE'VE LANDED THIS BULLSHIT MISSION?
YEAH, WE NEED TO MAKE A DISTRACTION JUST SO THIS FREAK CAN SNEAK INTO HÒN MÊ BY THE NORTH FACE!
THANKS FOR YOUR CONFIDENCE. TRY TO KEEP THE VIETS BUSY FOR AT LEAST THIRTY MINUTES...
?
JESUS, THE HELL IS HE DOING?

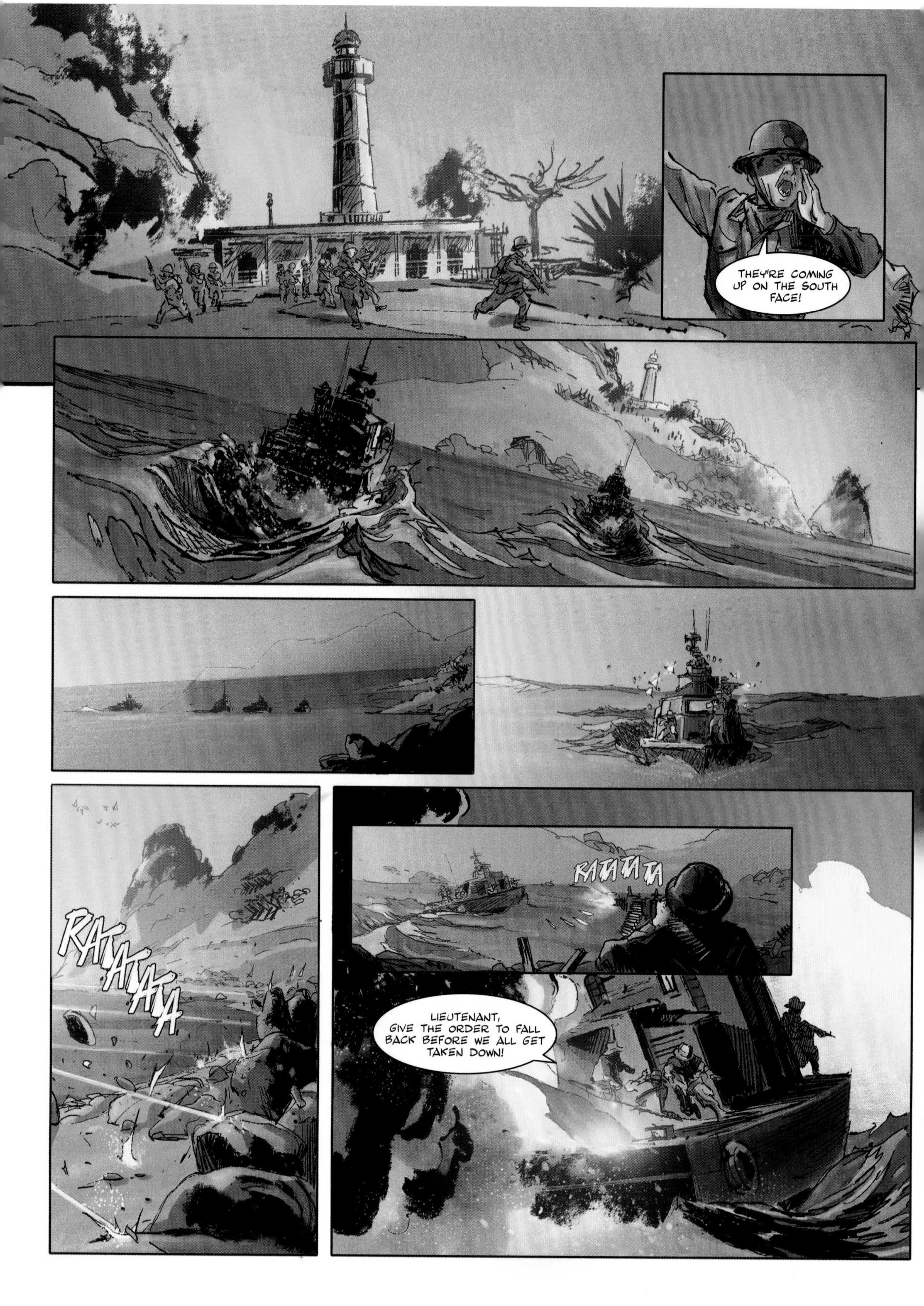
THEY'RE COMING UP ON THE SOUTH FACE!
RATATATA
RATATATA
LIEUTENANT, GIVE THE ORDER TO FALL BACK BEFORE WE ALL GET TAKEN DOWN!

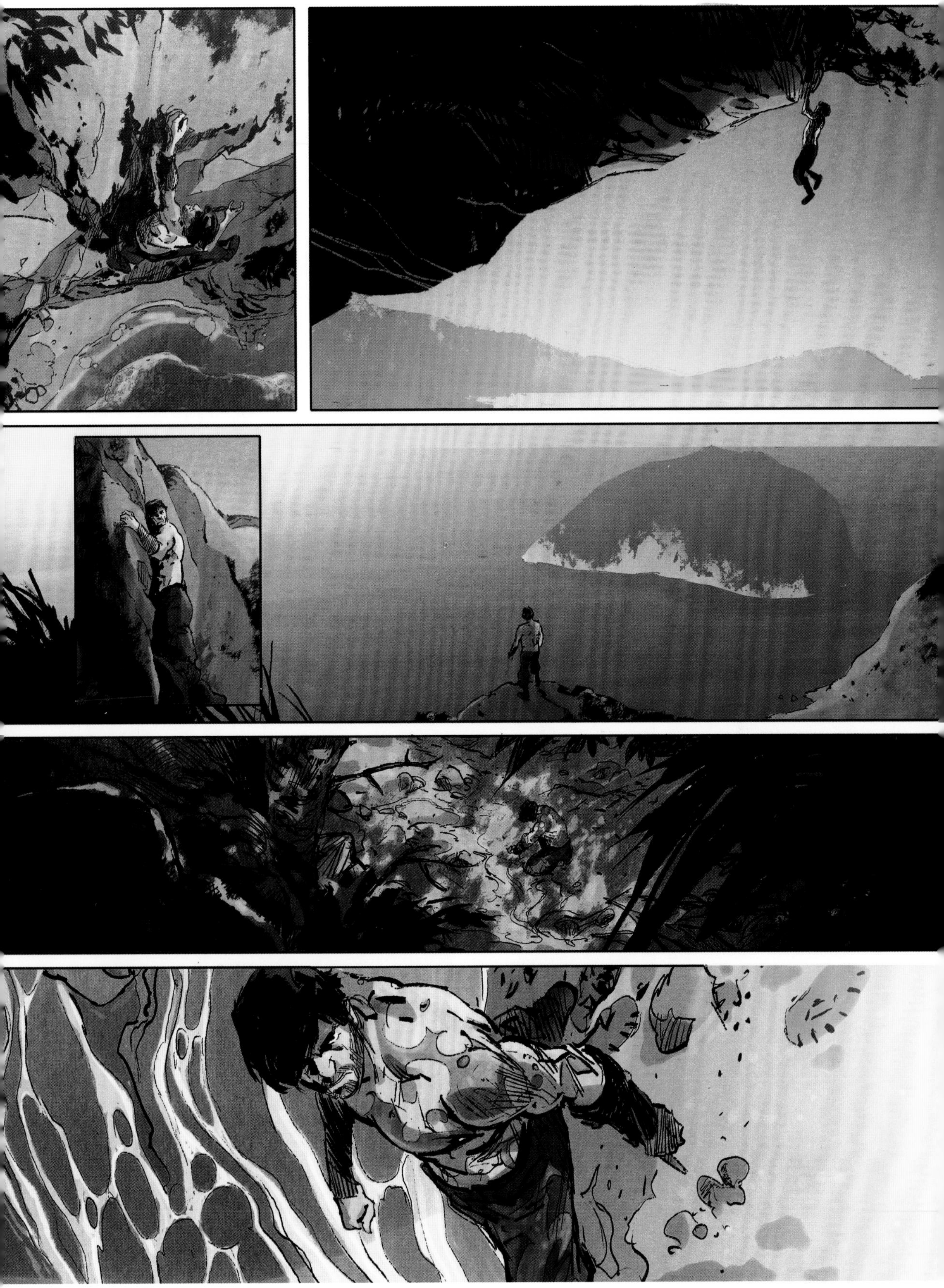

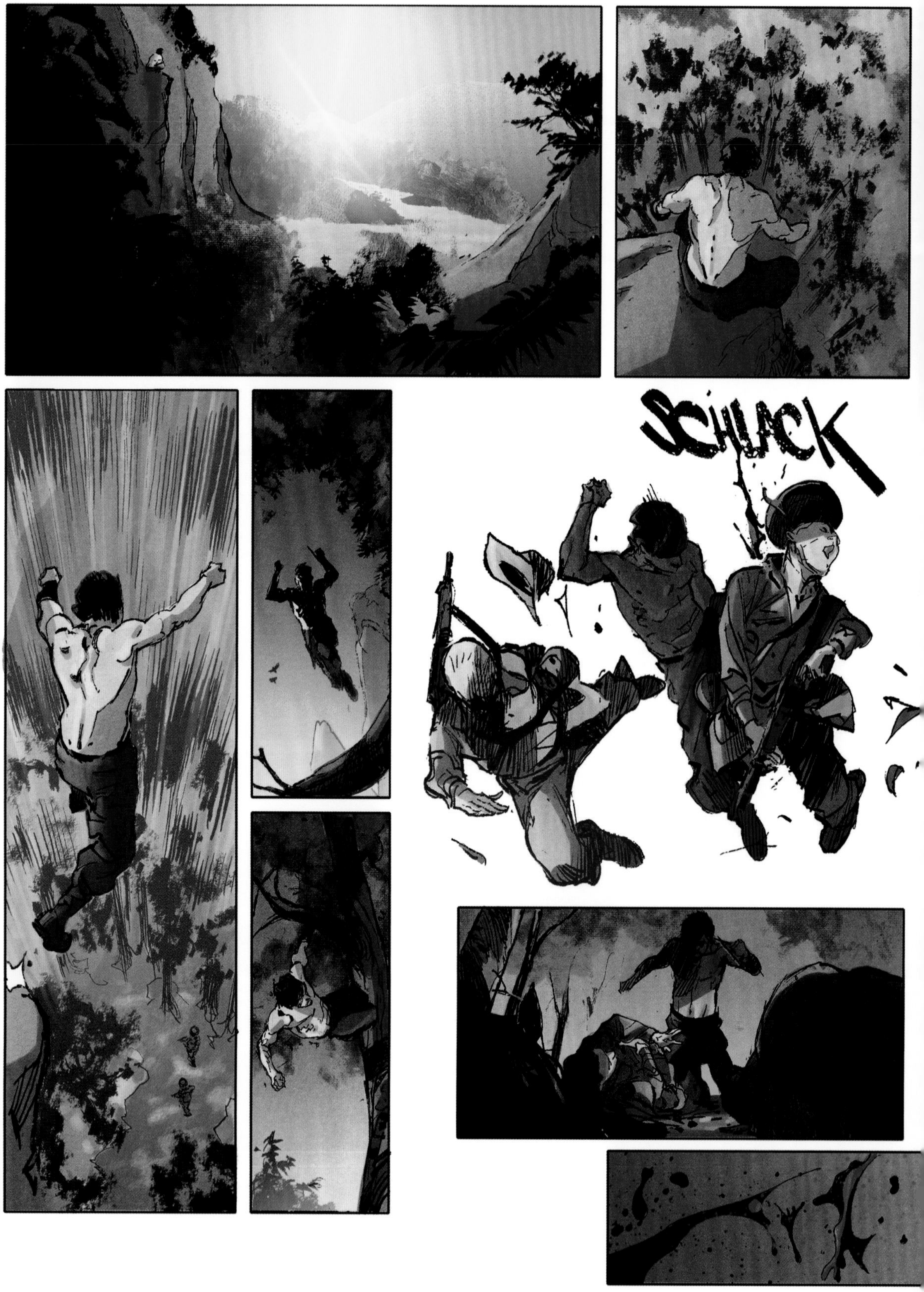
SCHLACK

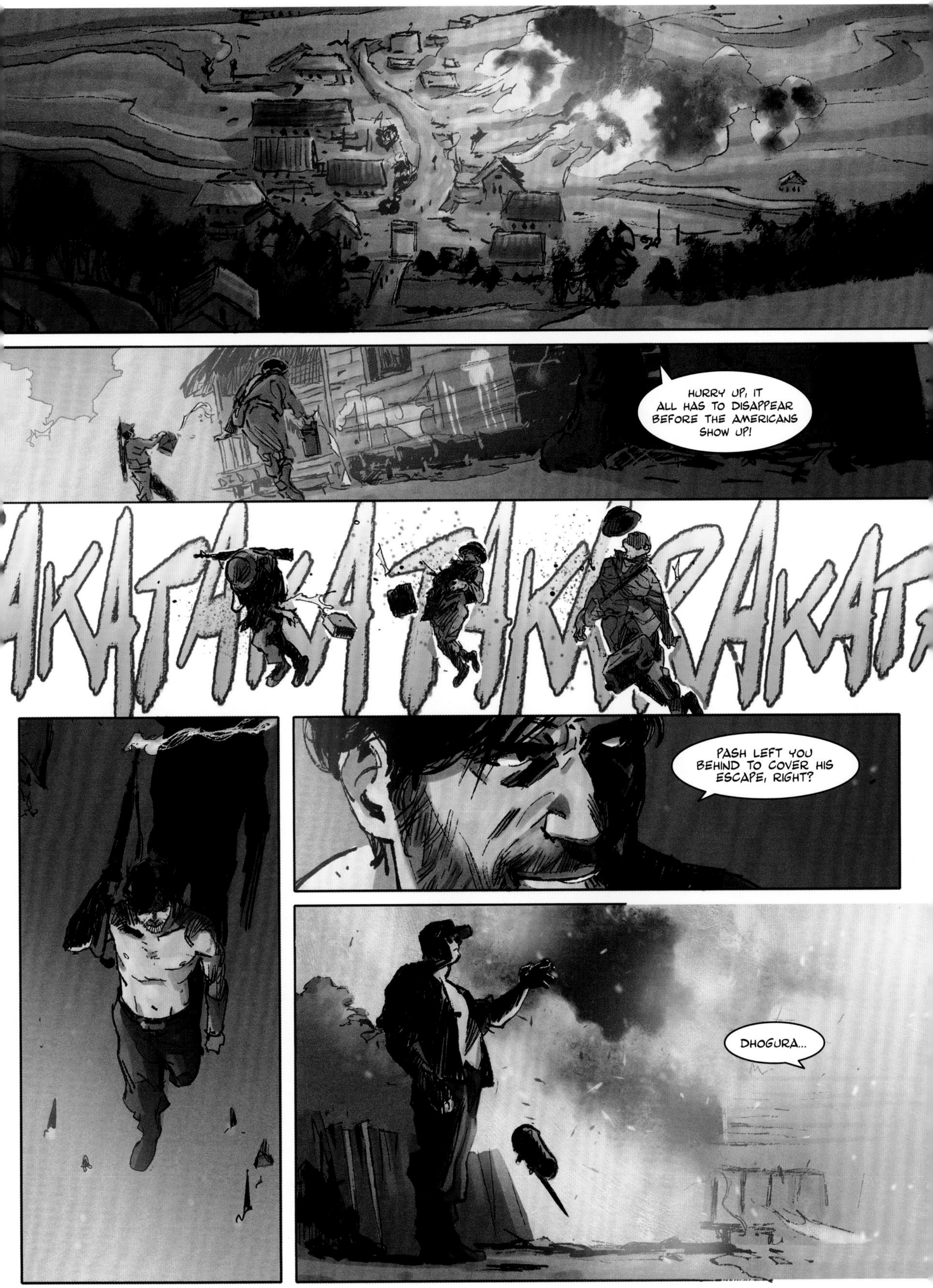
HURRY UP, IT ALL HAS TO DISAPPEAR BEFORE THE AMERICANS SHOW UP!
PASH LEFT YOU BEHIND TO COVER HIS ESCAPE, RIGHT?
DHOGURA...

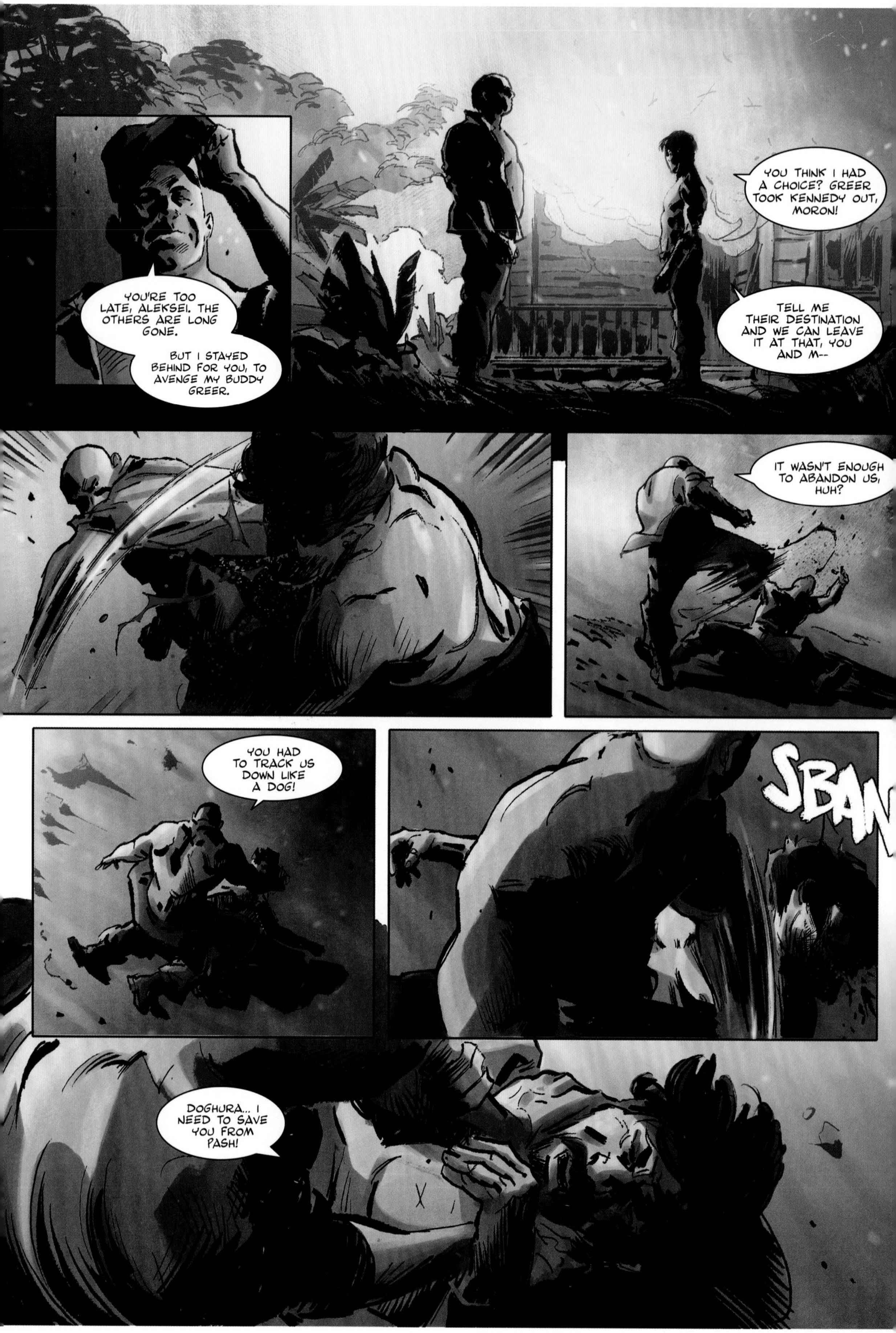
YOU'RE TOO LATE, ALEKSEI. THE OTHERS ARE LONG GONE.
BUT I STAYED BEHIND FOR YOU, TO AVENGE MY BUDDY GREER.
YOU THINK I HAD A CHOICE? GREER TOOK KENNEDY OUT, MORON!
TELL ME THEIR DESTINATION AND WE CAN LEAVE IT AT THAT, YOU AND M--
IT WASN'T ENOUGH TO ABANDON US, HUH?
YOU HAD TO TRACK US DOWN LIKE A DOG!
SBAN
DOGHURA... I NEED TO SAVE YOU FROM PASH!

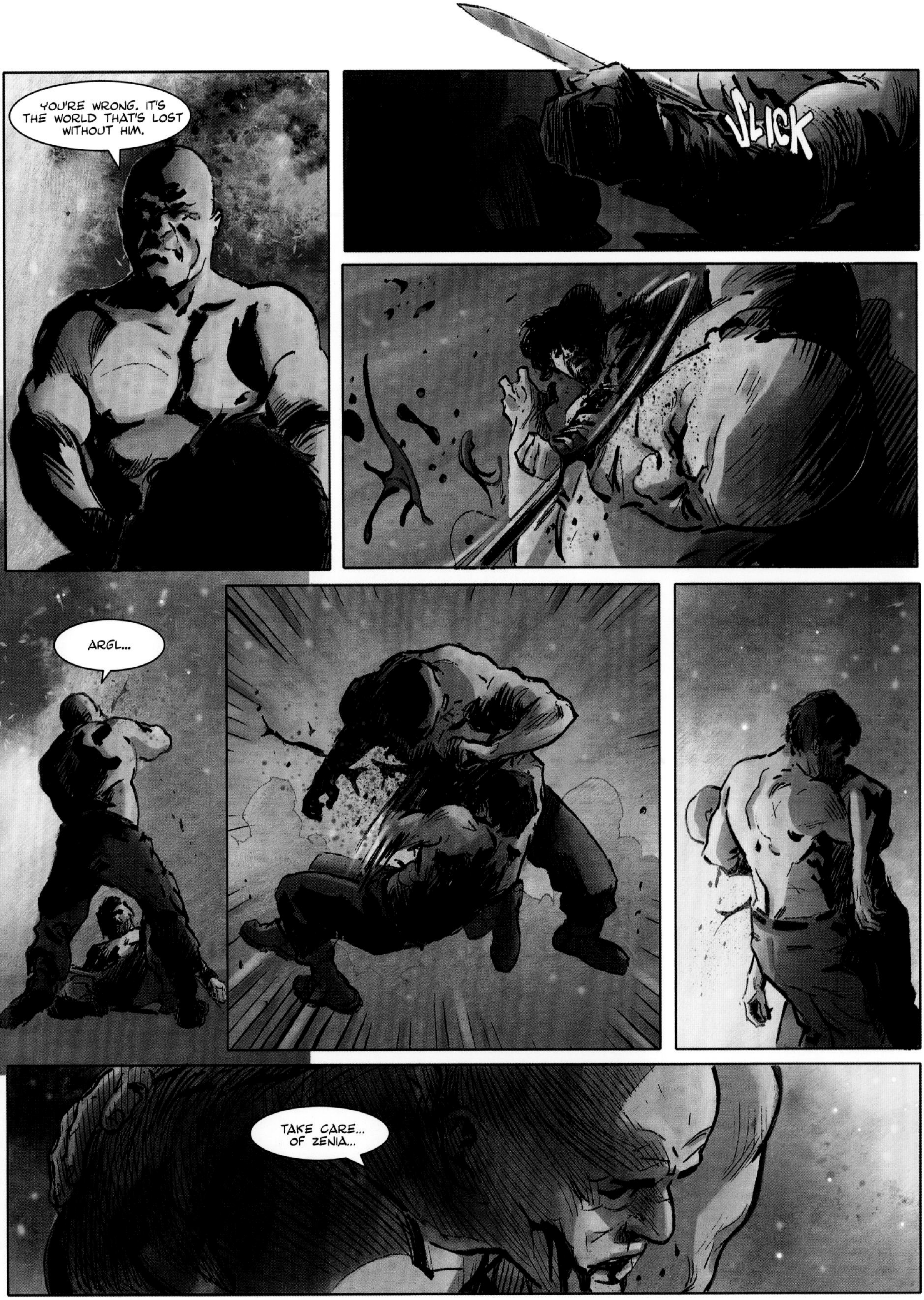
YOU'RE WRONG. IT'S THE WORLD THAT'S LOST WITHOUT HIM.
SLICK
ARGL...
TAKE CARE... OF ZENIA...

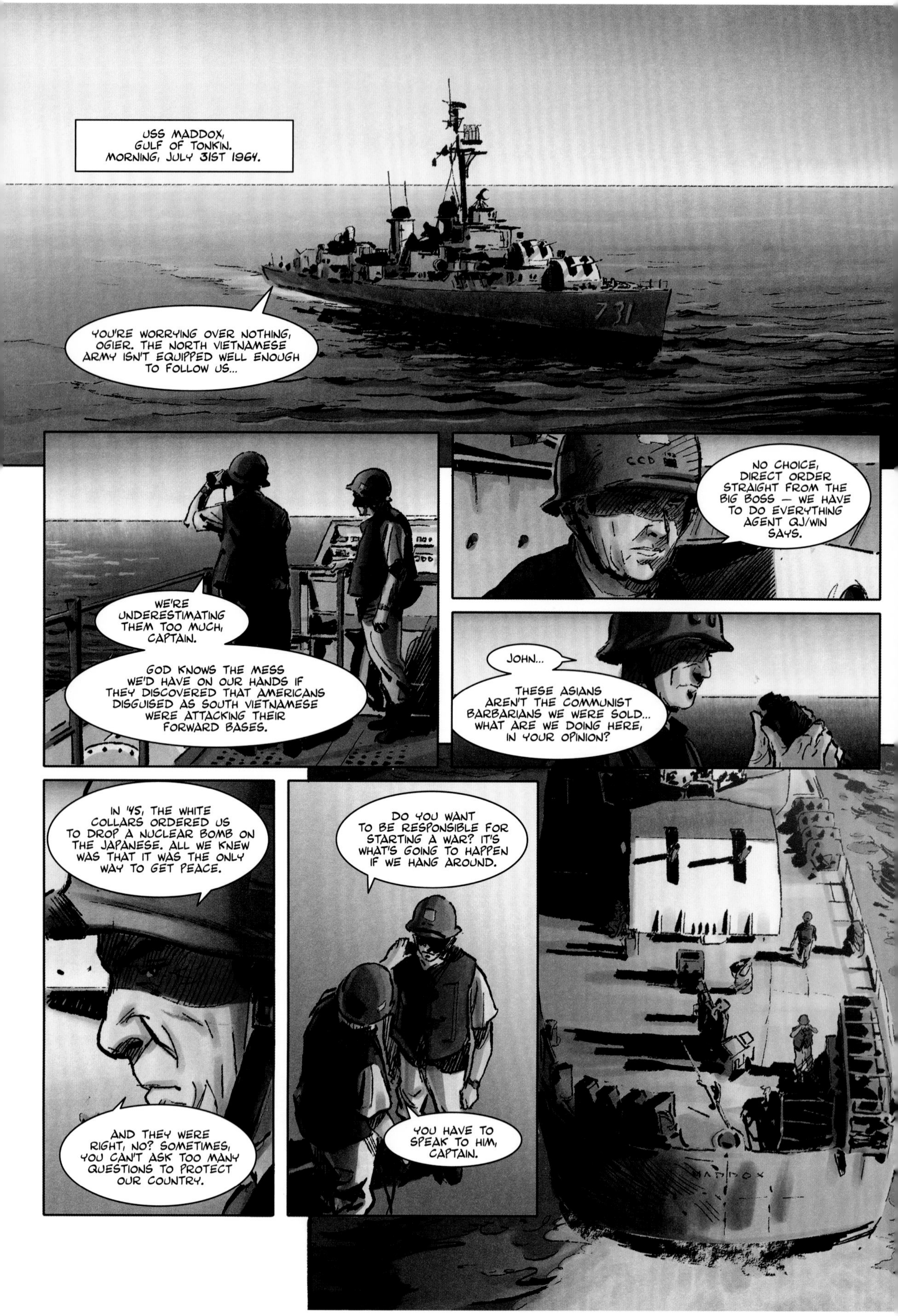
USS MADDOX, GULF OF TONKIN. MORNING, JULY 31ST 1964.
YOU'RE WORRYING OVER NOTHING, OGIER. THE NORTH VIETNAMESE ARMY ISN'T EQUIPPED WELL ENOUGH TO FOLLOW US...
WE'RE UNDERESTIMATING THEM TOO MUCH, CAPTAIN.
GOD KNOWS THE MESS WE'D HAVE ON OUR HANDS IF THEY DISCOVERED THAT AMERICANS DISGUISED AS SOUTH VIETNAMESE WERE ATTACKING THEIR FORWARD BASES.
NO CHOICE, DIRECT ORDER STRAIGHT FROM THE BIG BOSS — WE HAVE TO DO EVERYTHING AGENT QJ/WIN SAYS.
JOHN...
THESE ASIANS AREN'T THE COMMUNIST BARBARIANS WE WERE SOLD... WHAT ARE WE DOING HERE, IN YOUR OPINION?
IN '45, THE WHITE COLLARS ORDERED US TO DROP A NUCLEAR BOMB ON THE JAPANESE. ALL WE KNEW WAS THAT IT WAS THE ONLY WAY TO GET PEACE.
AND THEY WERE RIGHT, NO? SOMETIMES, YOU CAN'T ASK TOO MANY QUESTIONS TO PROTECT OUR COUNTRY.
DO YOU WANT TO BE RESPONSIBLE FOR STARTING A WAR? IT'S WHAT'S GOING TO HAPPEN IF WE HANG AROUND.
YOU HAVE TO SPEAK TO HIM, CAPTAIN.

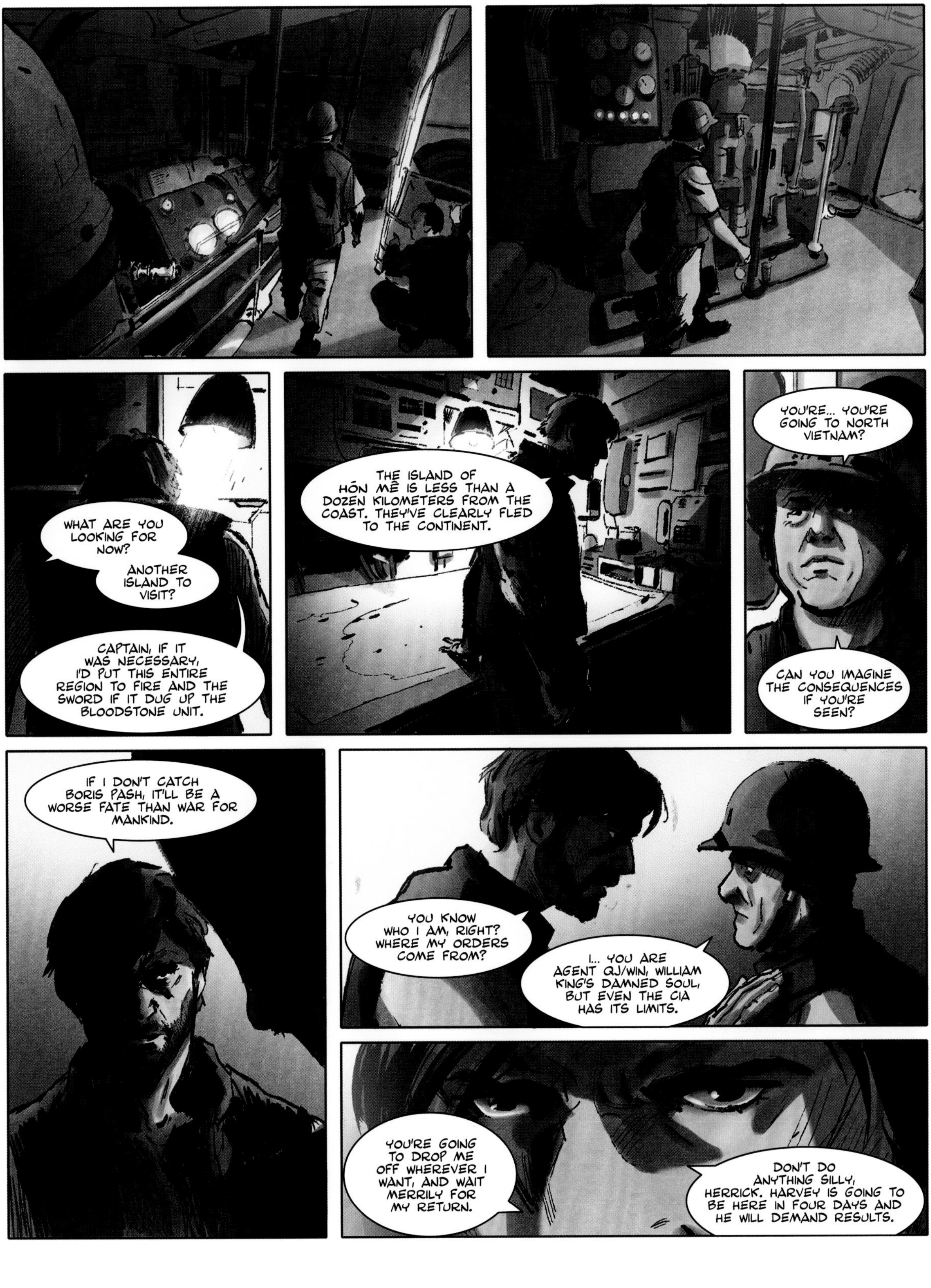
WHAT ARE YOU LOOKING FOR NOW?
ANOTHER ISLAND TO VISIT?
CAPTAIN, IF IT WAS NECESSARY, I'D PUT THIS ENTIRE REGION TO FIRE AND THE SWORD IF IT DUG UP THE BLOODSTONE UNIT.
THE ISLAND OF HÒN MÊ IS LESS THAN A DOZEN KILOMETERS FROM THE COAST. THEY'VE CLEARLY FLED TO THE CONTINENT.
YOU'RE... YOU'RE GOING TO NORTH VIETNAM?
CAN YOU IMAGINE THE CONSEQUENCES IF YOU'RE SEEN?
IF I DON'T CATCH BORIS PASH, IT'LL BE A WORSE FATE THAN WAR FOR MANKIND.
YOU KNOW WHO I AM, RIGHT? WHERE MY ORDERS COME FROM?
I... YOU ARE AGENT QJ/WIN, WILLIAM KING'S DAMNED SOUL, BUT EVEN THE CIA HAS ITS LIMITS.
YOU'RE GOING TO DROP ME OFF WHEREVER I WANT, AND WAIT MERRILY FOR MY RETURN.
DON'T DO ANYTHING SILLY, HERRICK. HARVEY IS GOING TO BE HERE IN FOUR DAYS AND HE WILL DEMAND RESULTS.

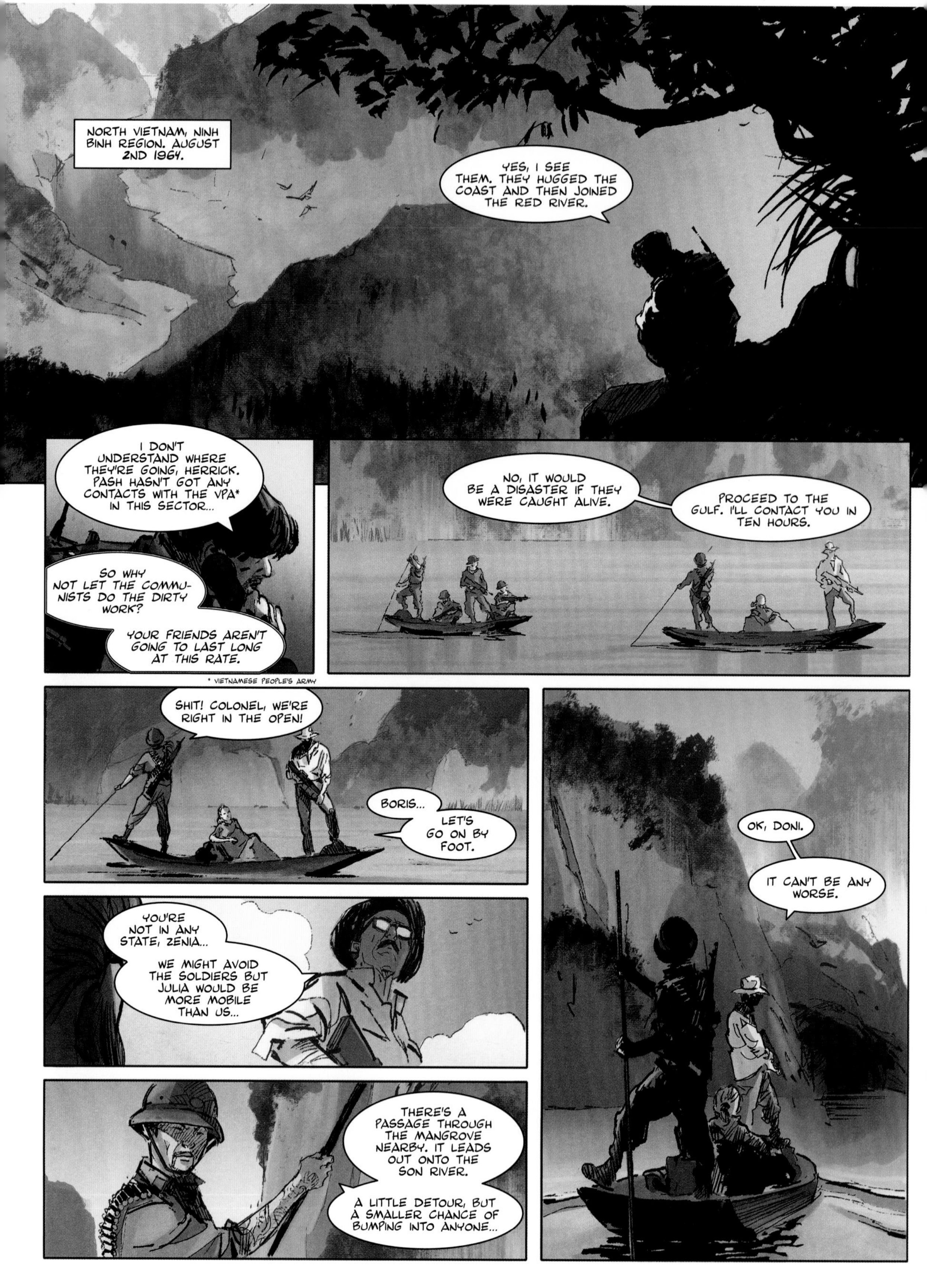
NORTH VIETNAM, NINH BINH REGION. AUGUST 2ND 1964.
YES, I SEE THEM. THEY HUGGED THE COAST AND THEN JOINED THE RED RIVER.
I DON'T UNDERSTAND WHERE THEY'RE GOING, HERRICK. PASH HASN'T GOT ANY CONTACTS WITH THE VPA* IN THIS SECTOR...
SO WHY NOT LET THE COMMUNISTS DO THE DIRTY WORK?
YOUR FRIENDS AREN'T GOING TO LAST LONG AT THIS RATE.
* VIETNAMESE PEOPLE'S ARMY
NO, IT WOULD BE A DISASTER IF THEY WERE CAUGHT ALIVE.
PROCEED TO THE GULF. I'LL CONTACT YOU IN TEN HOURS.
SHIT! COLONEL, WE'RE RIGHT IN THE OPEN!
BORIS...
LET'S GO ON BY FOOT.
YOU'RE NOT IN ANY STATE, ZENIA...
WE MIGHT AVOID THE SOLDIERS BUT JULIA WOULD BE MORE MOBILE THAN US...
THERE'S A PASSAGE THROUGH THE MANGROVE NEARBY. IT LEADS OUT ONTO THE SON RIVER.
A LITTLE DETOUR, BUT A SMALLER CHANCE OF BUMPING INTO ANYONE...
OK, DONI.
IT CAN'T BE ANY WORSE.

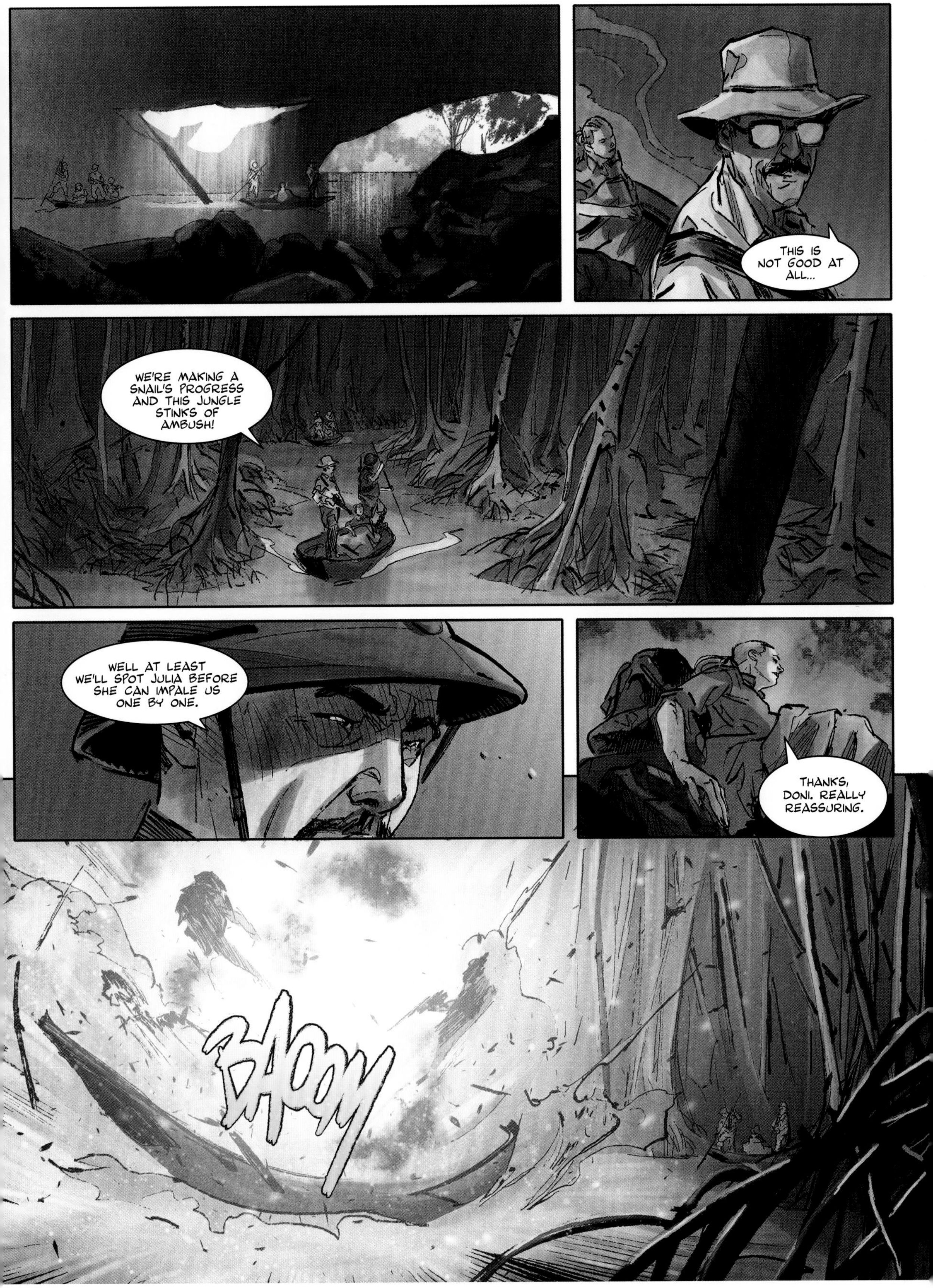
THIS IS NOT GOOD AT ALL...
WE'RE MAKING A SNAIL'S PROGRESS AND THIS JUNGLE STINKS OF AMBUSH!
WELL AT LEAST WE'LL SPOT JULIA BEFORE SHE CAN IMPALE US ONE BY ONE.
THANKS, DONI. REALLY REASSURING.
BAOOM

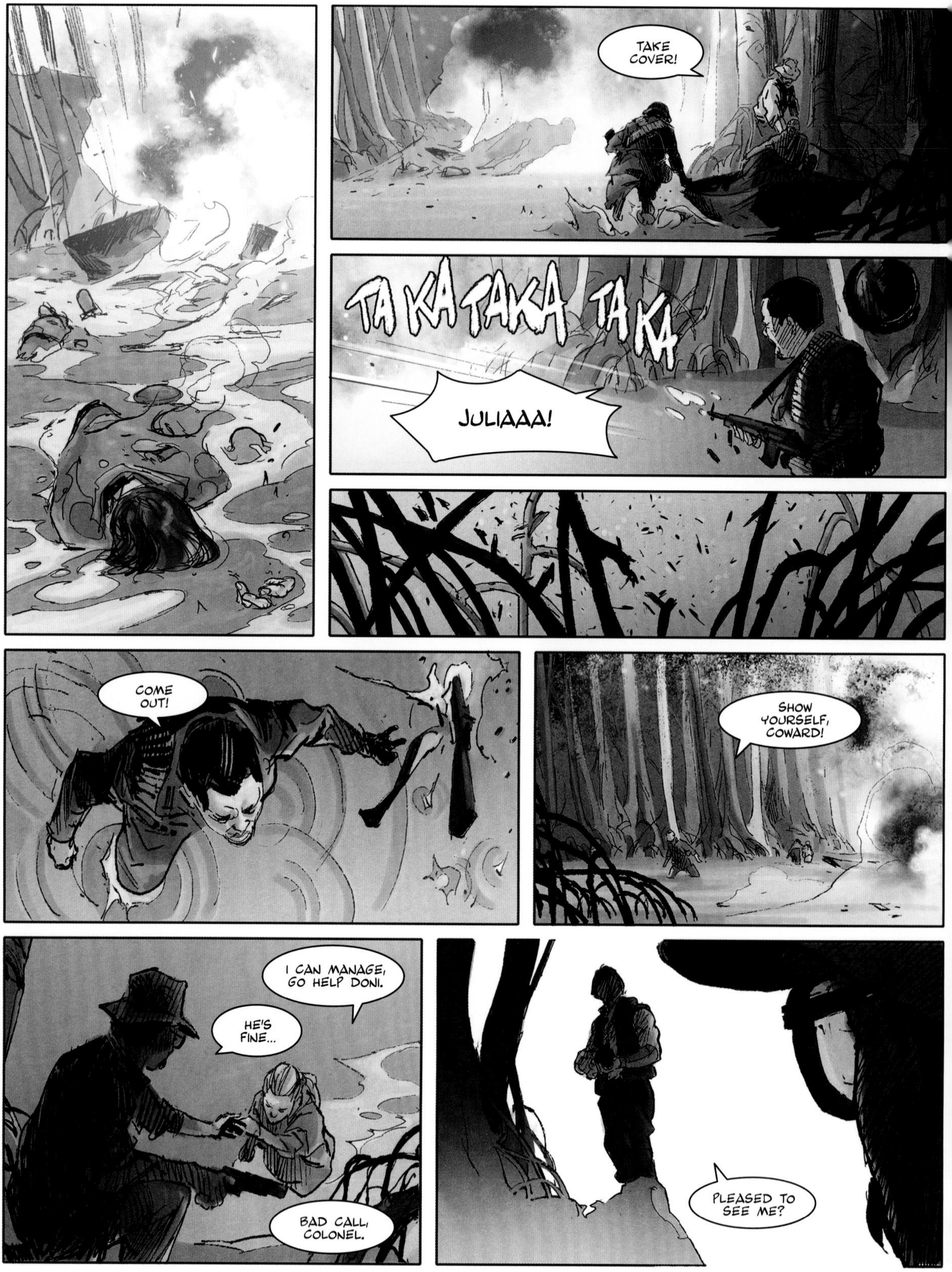
TAKE COVER!
TA KA TAKA TA KA
JULIAAA!
COME OUT!
SHOW YOURSELF, COWARD!
I CAN MANAGE, GO HELP DONI.
HE'S FINE...
BAD CALL, COLONEL.
PLEASED TO SEE ME?

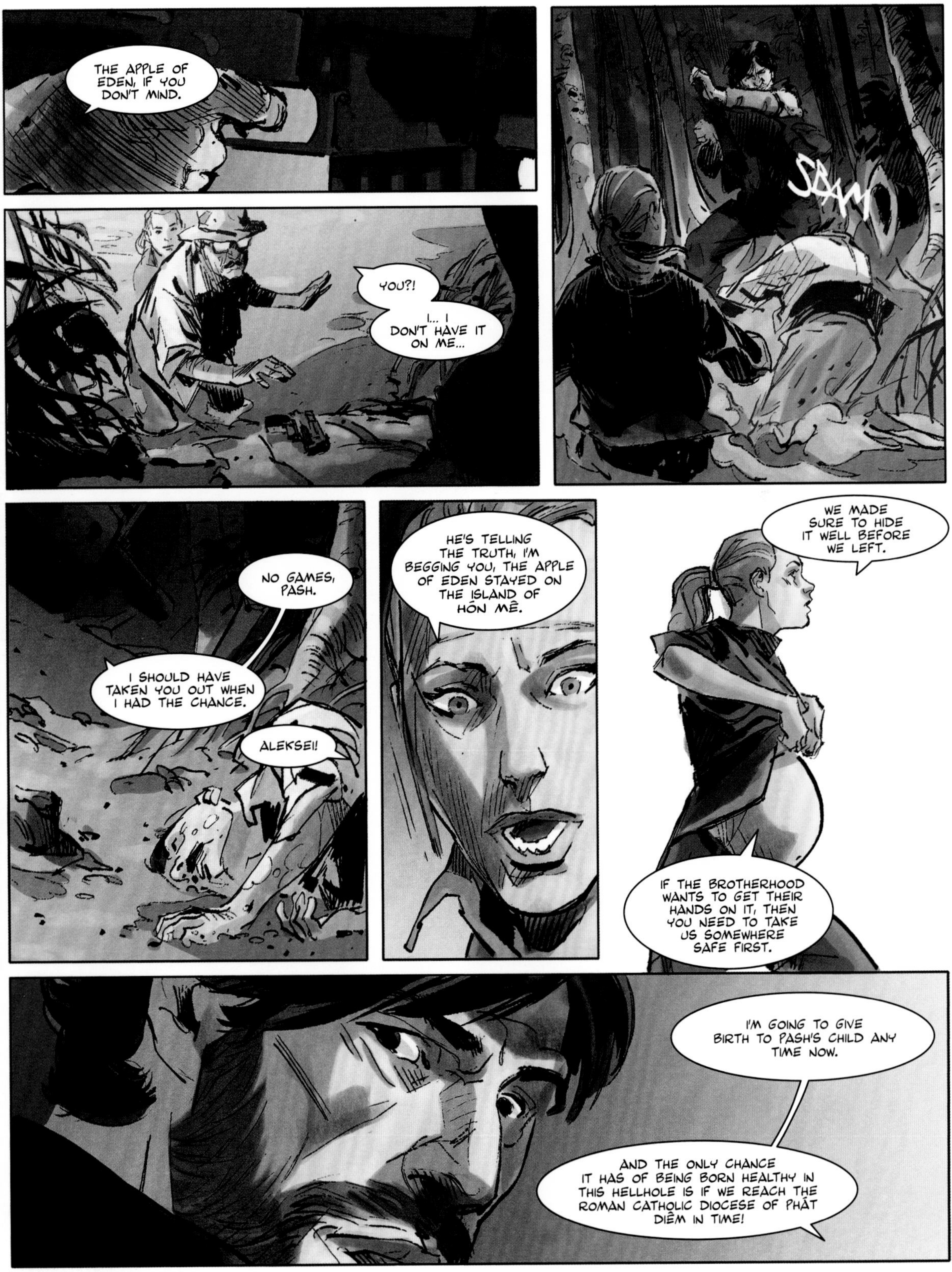
THE APPLE OF EDEN, IF YOU DON'T MIND.
YOU?!
I... I DON'T HAVE IT ON ME...
SBAM
NO GAMES, PASH.
I SHOULD HAVE TAKEN YOU OUT WHEN I HAD THE CHANCE.
ALEKSEI!
HE'S TELLING THE TRUTH, I'M BEGGING YOU, THE APPLE OF EDEN STAYED ON THE ISLAND OF HÒN MÊ.
WE MADE SURE TO HIDE IT WELL BEFORE WE LEFT.
IF THE BROTHERHOOD WANTS TO GET THEIR HANDS ON IT, THEN YOU NEED TO TAKE US SOMEWHERE SAFE FIRST.
I'M GOING TO GIVE BIRTH TO PASH'S CHILD ANY TIME NOW.
AND THE ONLY CHANCE IT HAS OF BEING BORN HEALTHY IN THIS HELLHOLE IS IF WE REACH THE ROMAN CATHOLIC DIOCESE OF PHÁT DIÊM IN TIME!

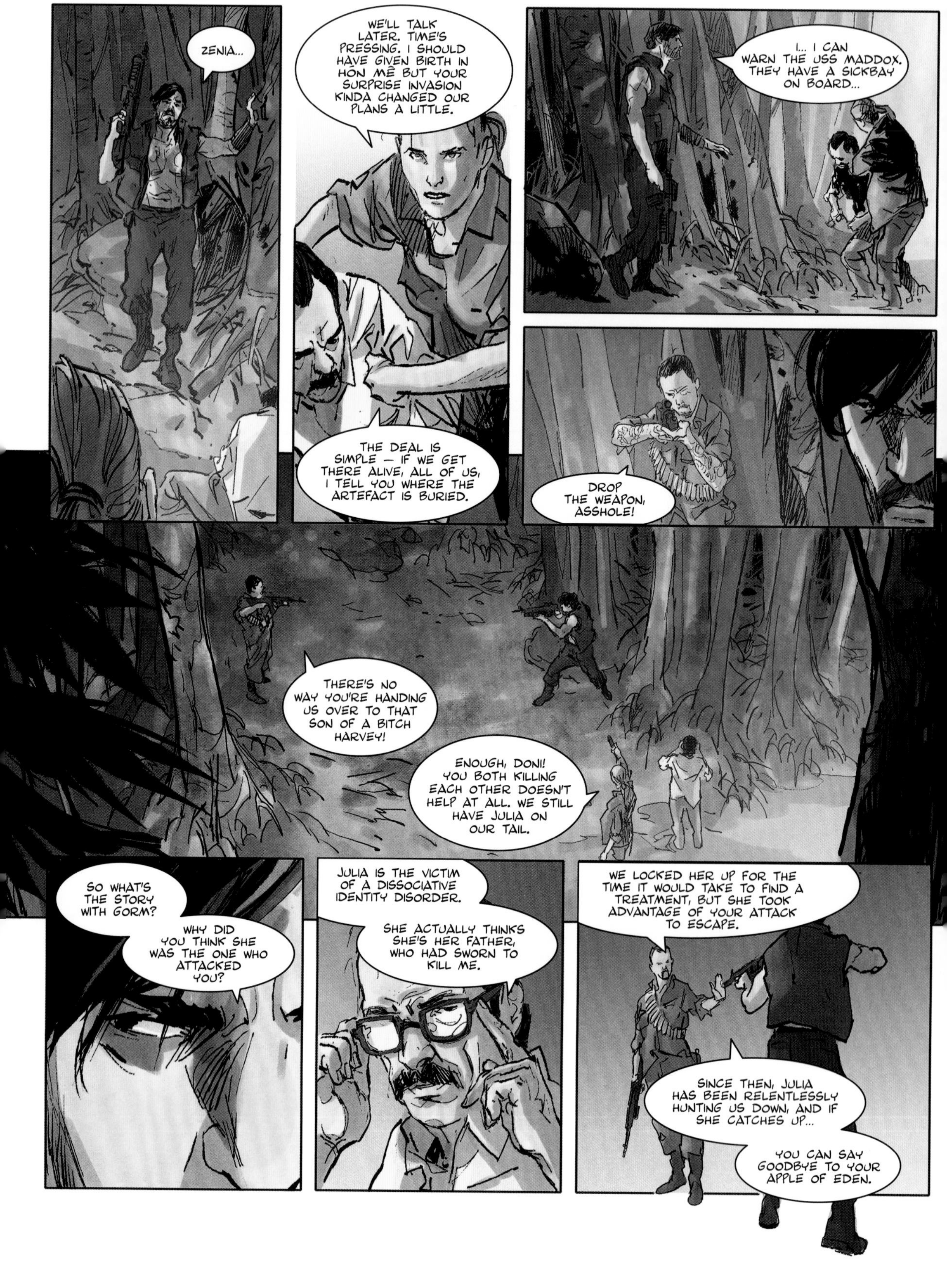
ZENIA...
WE'LL TALK LATER. TIME'S PRESSING. I SHOULD HAVE GIVEN BIRTH IN HÒN MÊ BUT YOUR SURPRISE INVASION KINDA CHANGED OUR PLANS A LITTLE.
THE DEAL IS SIMPLE — IF WE GET THERE ALIVE, ALL OF US, I TELL YOU WHERE THE ARTEFACT IS BURIED.
I... I CAN WARN THE USS MADDOX. THEY HAVE A SICKBAY ON BOARD...
DROP THE WEAPON, ASSHOLE!
THERE'S NO WAY YOU'RE HANDING US OVER TO THAT SON OF A BITCH HARVEY!
ENOUGH, DONI! YOU BOTH KILLING EACH OTHER DOESN'T HELP AT ALL. WE STILL HAVE JULIA ON OUR TAIL.
SO WHAT'S THE STORY WITH GORM?
WHY DID YOU THINK SHE WAS THE ONE WHO ATTACKED YOU?
JULIA IS THE VICTIM OF A DISSOCIATIVE IDENTITY DISORDER.
SHE ACTUALLY THINKS SHE'S HER FATHER, WHO HAD SWORN TO KILL ME.
WE LOCKED HER UP FOR THE TIME IT WOULD TAKE TO FIND A TREATMENT, BUT SHE TOOK ADVANTAGE OF YOUR ATTACK TO ESCAPE.
SINCE THEN, JULIA HAS BEEN RELENTLESSLY HUNTING US DOWN, AND IF SHE CATCHES UP...
YOU CAN SAY GOODBYE TO YOUR APPLE OF EDEN.

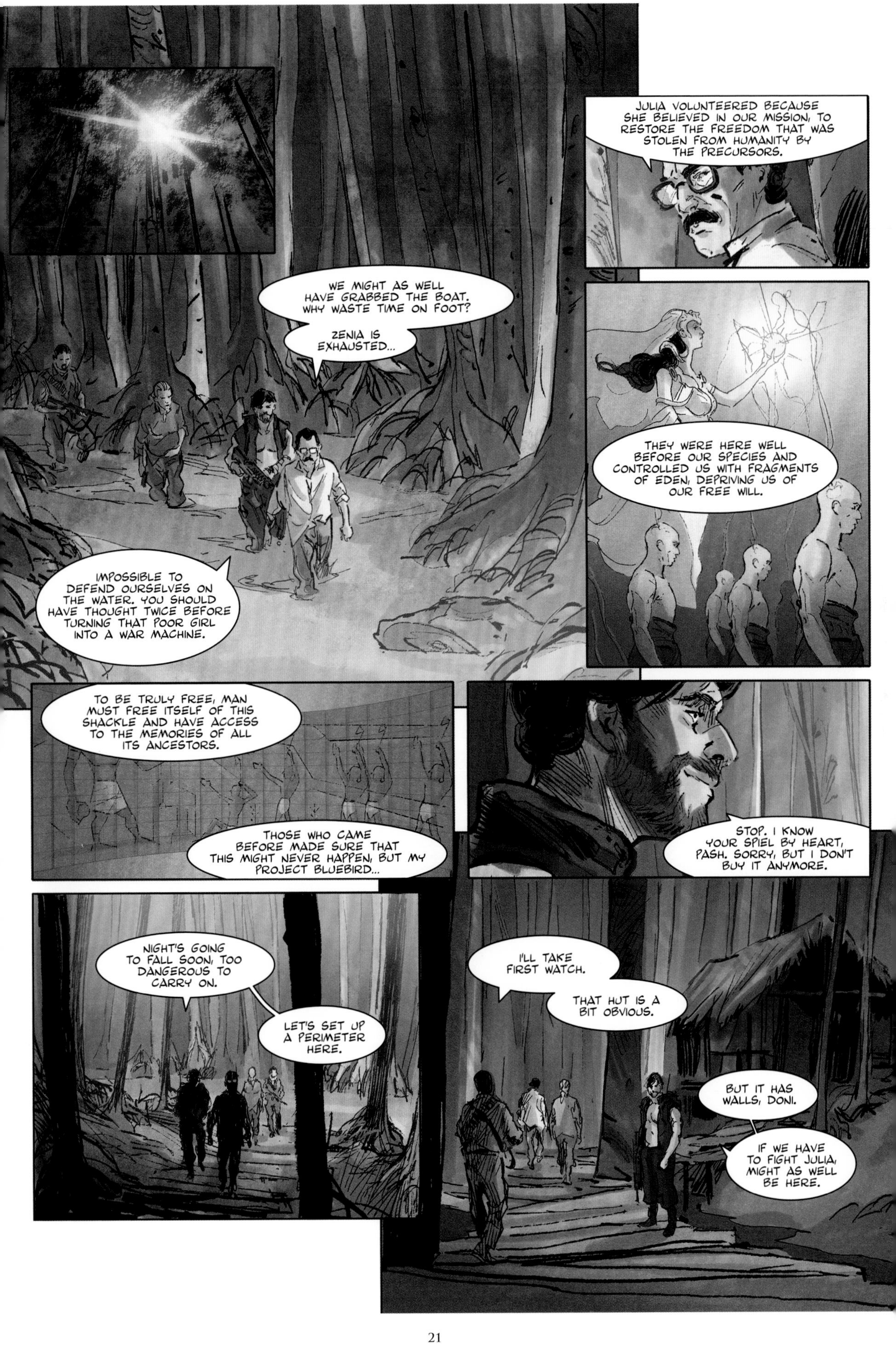
JULIA VOLUNTEERED BECAUSE SHE BELIEVED IN OUR MISSION, TO RESTORE THE FREEDOM THAT WAS STOLEN FROM HUMANITY BY THE PRECURSORS.
WE MIGHT AS WELL HAVE GRABBED THE BOAT. WHY WASTE TIME ON FOOT?
ZENIA IS EXHAUSTED...
IMPOSSIBLE TO DEFEND OURSELVES ON THE WATER. YOU SHOULD HAVE THOUGHT TWICE BEFORE TURNING THAT POOR GIRL INTO A WAR MACHINE.
THEY WERE HERE WELL BEFORE OUR SPECIES AND CONTROLLED US WITH FRAGMENTS OF EDEN, DEPRIVING US OF OUR FREE WILL.
TO BE TRULY FREE, MAN MUST FREE ITSELF OF THIS SHACKLE AND HAVE ACCESS TO THE MEMORIES OF ALL ITS ANCESTORS.
THOSE WHO CAME BEFORE MADE SURE THAT THIS MIGHT NEVER HAPPEN, BUT MY PROJECT BLUEBIRD...
STOP. I KNOW YOUR SPIEL BY HEART, PASH. SORRY, BUT I DON'T BUY IT ANYMORE.
NIGHT'S GOING TO FALL SOON, TOO DANGEROUS TO CARRY ON.
LET'S SET UP A PERIMETER HERE.
I'LL TAKE FIRST WATCH.
THAT HUT IS A BIT OBVIOUS.
BUT IT HAS WALLS, DONI.
IF WE HAVE TO FIGHT JULIA, MIGHT AS WELL BE HERE.

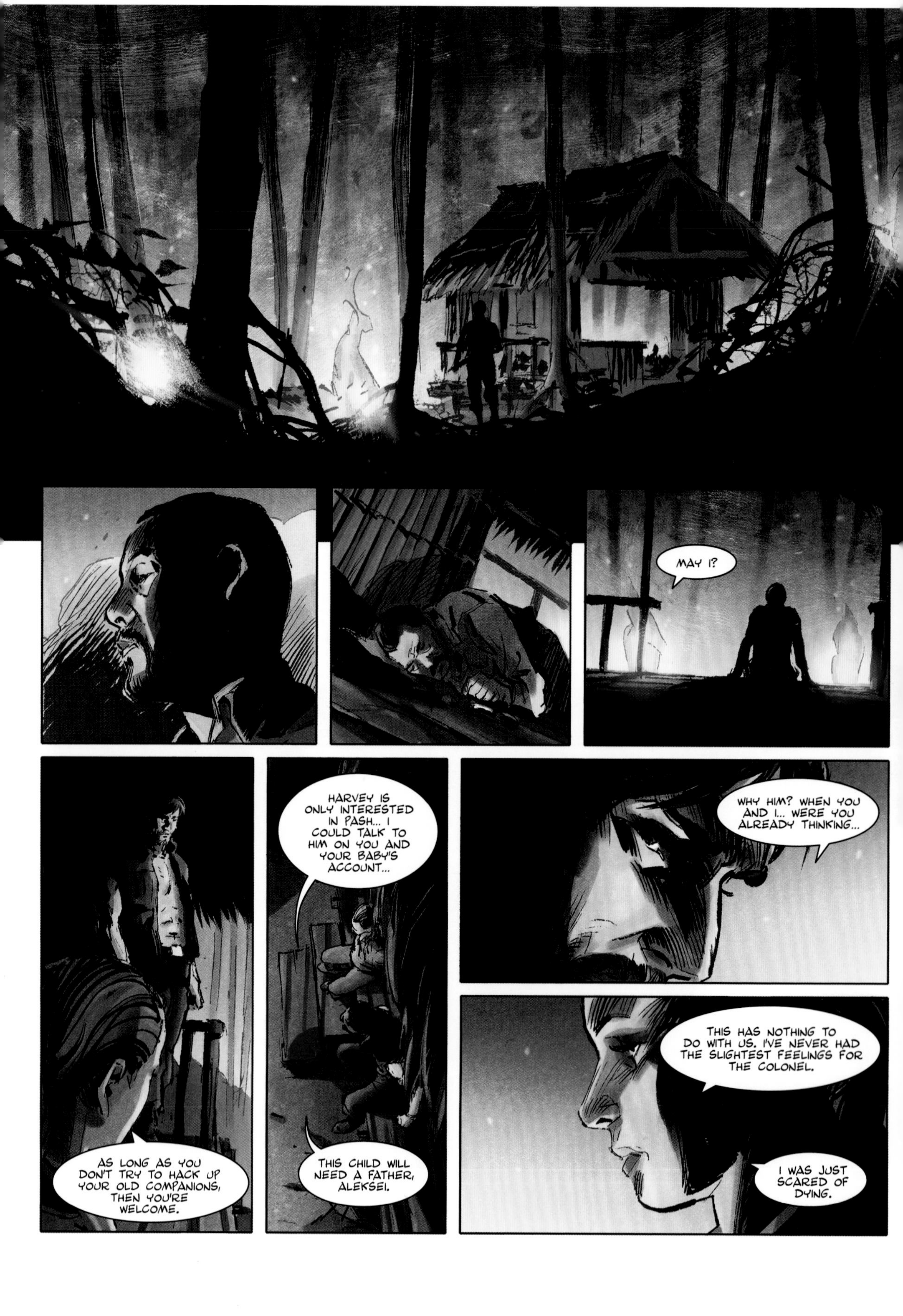

MAY I?
AS LONG AS YOU DON'T TRY TO HACK UP YOUR OLD COMPANIONS, THEN YOU'RE WELCOME.
HARVEY IS ONLY INTERESTED IN PASH... I COULD TALK TO HIM ON YOU AND YOUR BABY'S ACCOUNT...
THIS CHILD WILL NEED A FATHER, ALEKSEI.
WHY HIM? WHEN YOU AND I... WERE YOU ALREADY THINKING...
THIS HAS NOTHING TO DO WITH US. I'VE NEVER HAD THE SLIGHTEST FEELINGS FOR THE COLONEL.
I WAS JUST SCARED OF DYING.

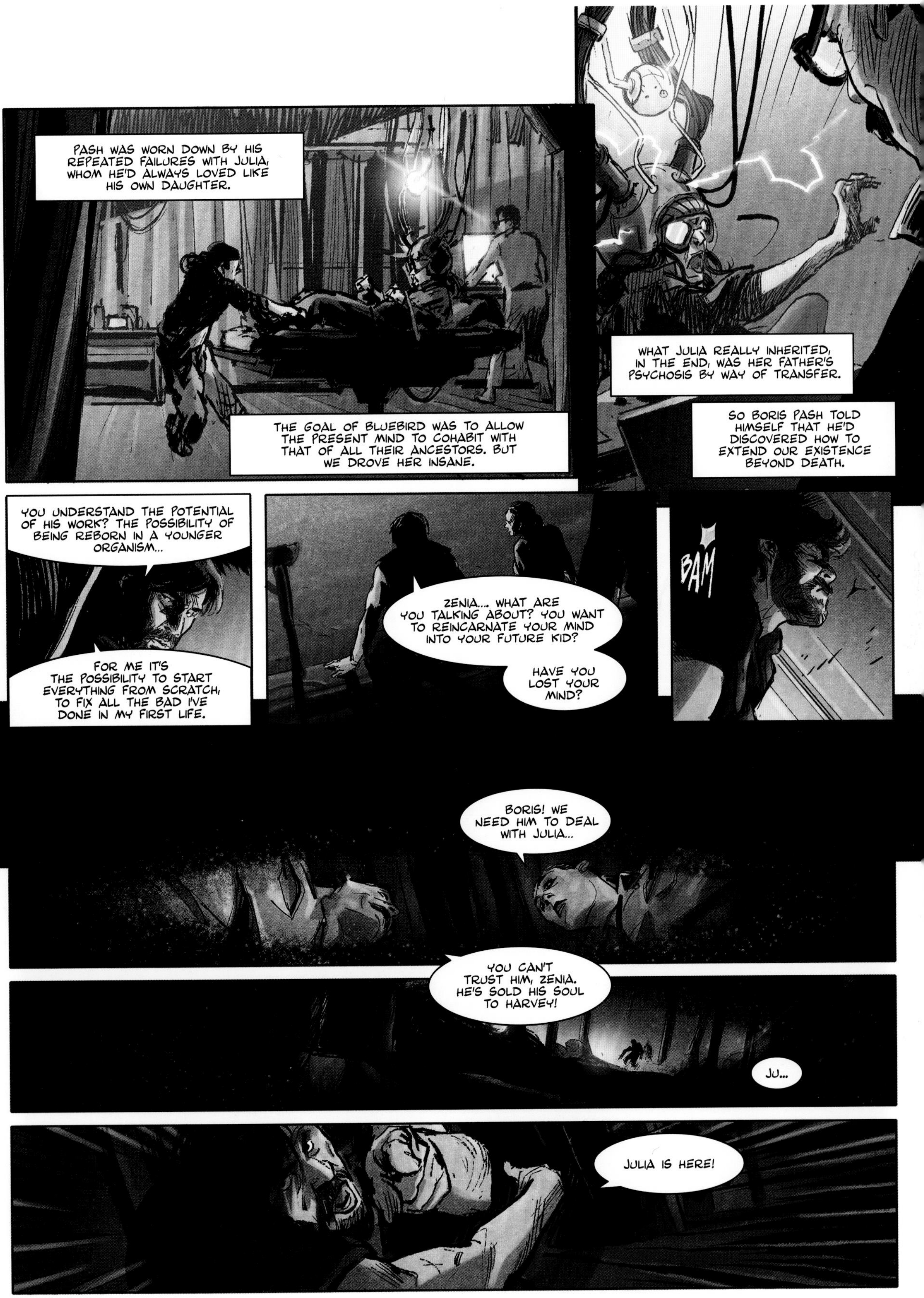
PASH WAS WORN DOWN BY HIS REPEATED FAILURES WITH JULIA, WHOM HE'D ALWAYS LOVED LIKE HIS OWN DAUGHTER.
THE GOAL OF BLUEBIRD WAS TO ALLOW THE PRESENT MIND TO COHABIT WITH THAT OF ALL THEIR ANCESTORS. BUT WE DROVE HER INSANE.
WHAT JULIA REALLY INHERITED, IN THE END, WAS HER FATHER'S PSYCHOSIS BY WAY OF TRANSFER.
SO BORIS PASH TOLD HIMSELF THAT HE'D DISCOVERED HOW TO EXTEND OUR EXISTENCE BEYOND DEATH.
YOU UNDERSTAND THE POTENTIAL OF HIS WORK? THE POSSIBILITY OF BEING REBORN IN A YOUNGER ORGANISM...
FOR ME IT'S THE POSSIBILITY TO START EVERYTHING FROM SCRATCH, TO FIX ALL THE BAD I'VE DONE IN MY FIRST LIFE.
ZENIA... WHAT ARE YOU TALKING ABOUT? YOU WANT TO REINCARNATE YOUR MIND INTO YOUR FUTURE KID?
HAVE YOU LOST YOUR MIND?
BAM
BORIS! WE NEED HIM TO DEAL WITH JULIA...
YOU CAN'T TRUST HIM, ZENIA. HE'S SOLD HIS SOUL TO HARVEY!
JU...
JULIA IS HERE!

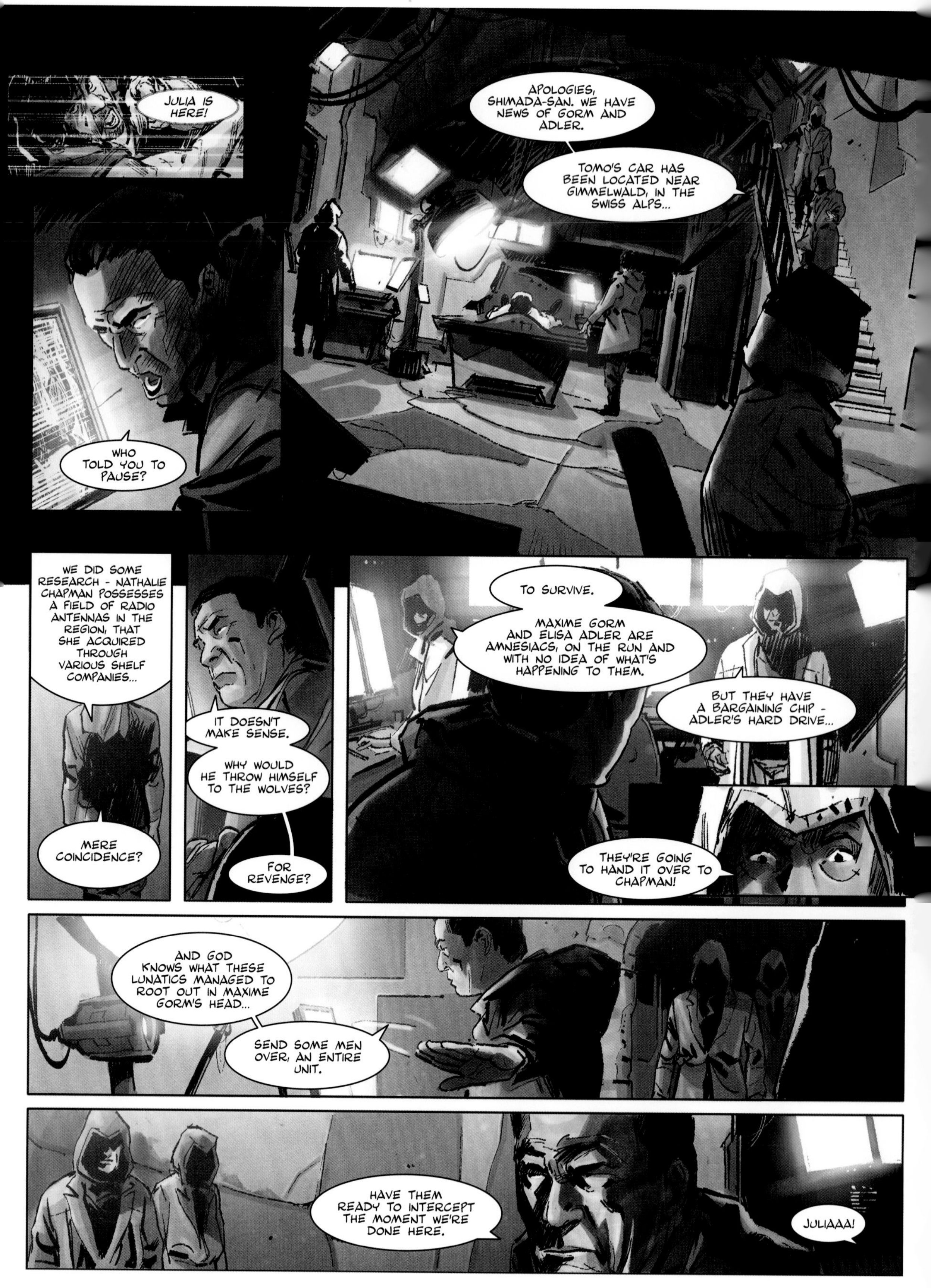
JULIA IS HERE!
WHO TOLD YOU TO PAUSE?
APOLOGIES, SHIMADA-SAN. WE HAVE NEWS OF GORM AND ADLER.
TOMO'S CAR HAS BEEN LOCATED NEAR GIMMELWALD, IN THE SWISS ALPS...
WE DID SOME RESEARCH - NATHALIE CHAPMAN POSSESSES A FIELD OF RADIO ANTENNAS IN THE REGION, THAT SHE ACQUIRED THROUGH VARIOUS SHELF COMPANIES...
MERE COINCIDENCE?
IT DOESN'T MAKE SENSE.
WHY WOULD HE THROW HIMSELF TO THE WOLVES?
FOR REVENGE?
TO SURVIVE.
MAXIME GORM AND ELISA ADLER ARE AMNESIACS, ON THE RUN AND WITH NO IDEA OF WHAT'S HAPPENING TO THEM.
BUT THEY HAVE A BARGAINING CHIP - ADLER'S HARD DRIVE...
THEY'RE GOING TO HAND IT OVER TO CHAPMAN!
AND GOD KNOWS WHAT THESE LUNATICS MANAGED TO ROOT OUT IN MAXIME GORM'S HEAD...
SEND SOME MEN OVER, AN ENTIRE UNIT.
HAVE THEM READY TO INTERCEPT THE MOMENT WE'RE DONE HERE.
JULIAAA!

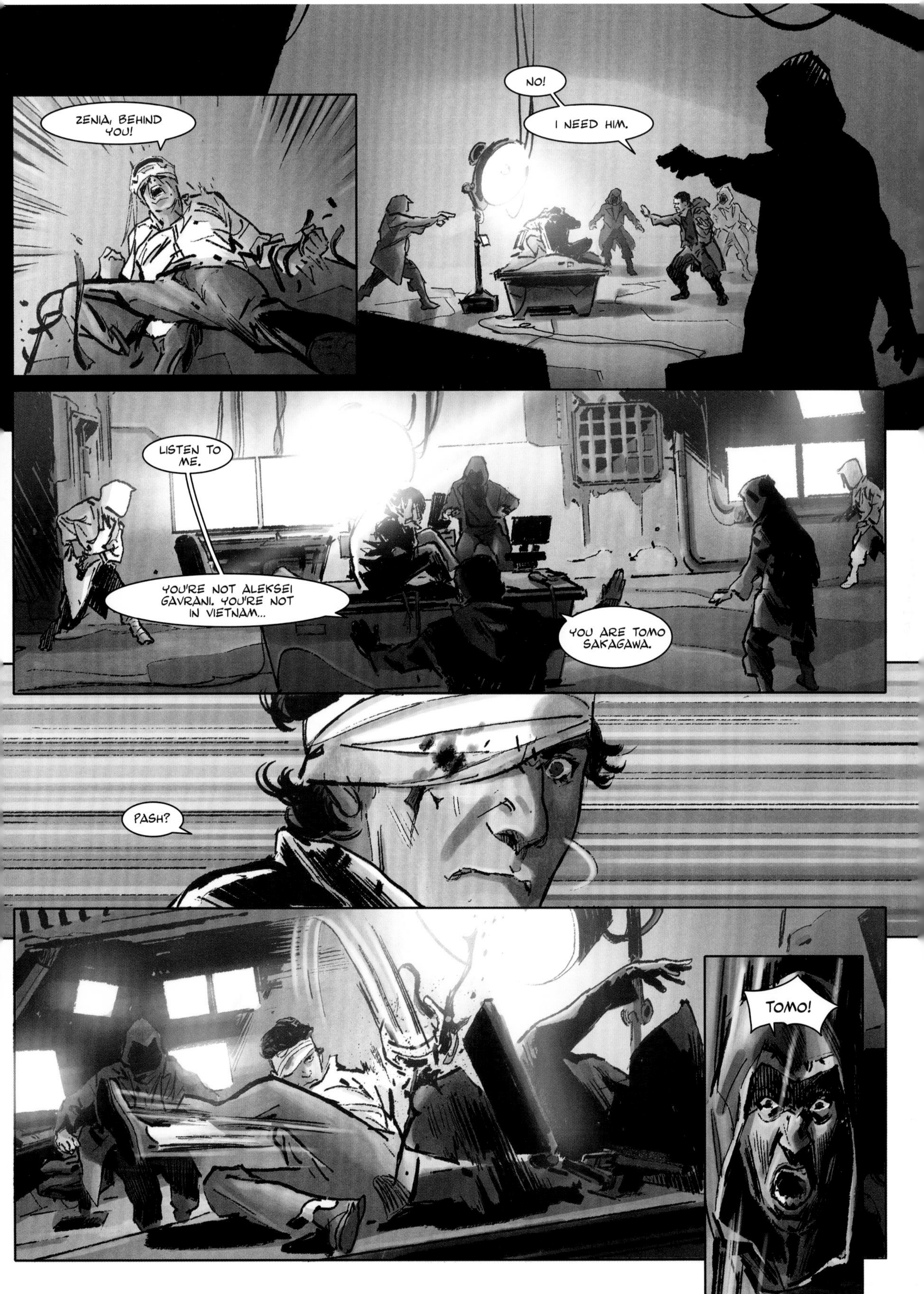

ZENIA, BEHIND YOU!
NO!
I NEED HIM.
LISTEN TO ME.
YOU'RE NOT ALEKSEI GAVRANI. YOU'RE NOT IN VIETNAM...
YOU ARE TOMO SAKAGAWA.
PASH?
TOMO!

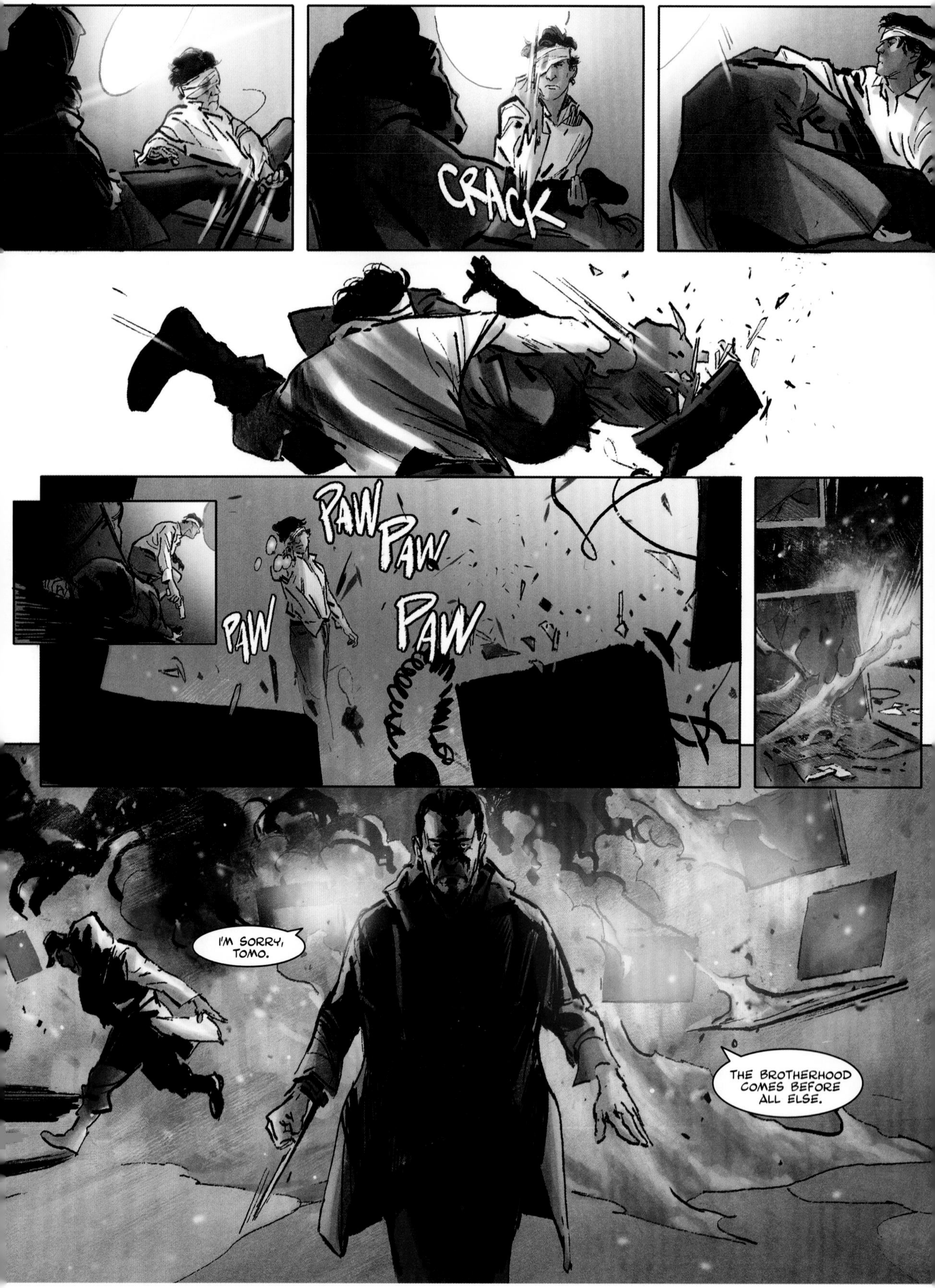
CRACK
PAW
PAW
PAW
PAW
I'M SORRY, TOMO.
THE BROTHERHOOD COMES BEFORE ALL ELSE.

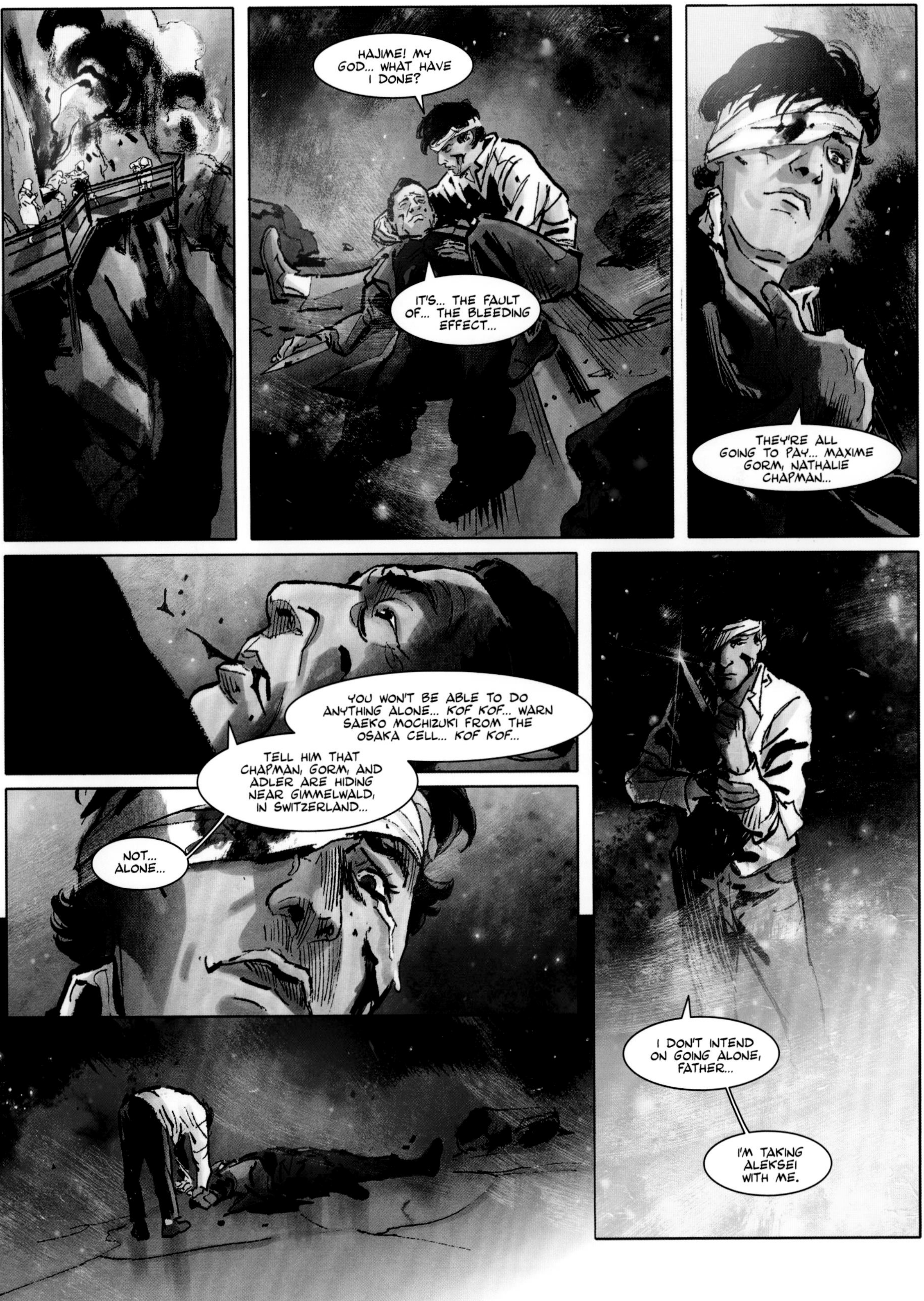
HAJIME! MY GOD... WHAT HAVE I DONE?
IT'S... THE FAULT OF... THE BLEEDING EFFECT...
THEY'RE ALL GOING TO PAY... MAXIME GORM, NATHALIE CHAPMAN...
YOU WON'T BE ABLE TO DO ANYTHING ALONE... KOF KOF... WARN SAEKO MOCHIZUKI FROM THE OSAKA CELL... KOF KOF...
TELL HIM THAT CHAPMAN, GORM, AND ADLER ARE HIDING NEAR GIMMELWALD, IN SWITZERLAND...
NOT... ALONE...
I DON'T INTEND ON GOING ALONE, FATHER...
I'M TAKING ALEKSEI WITH ME.

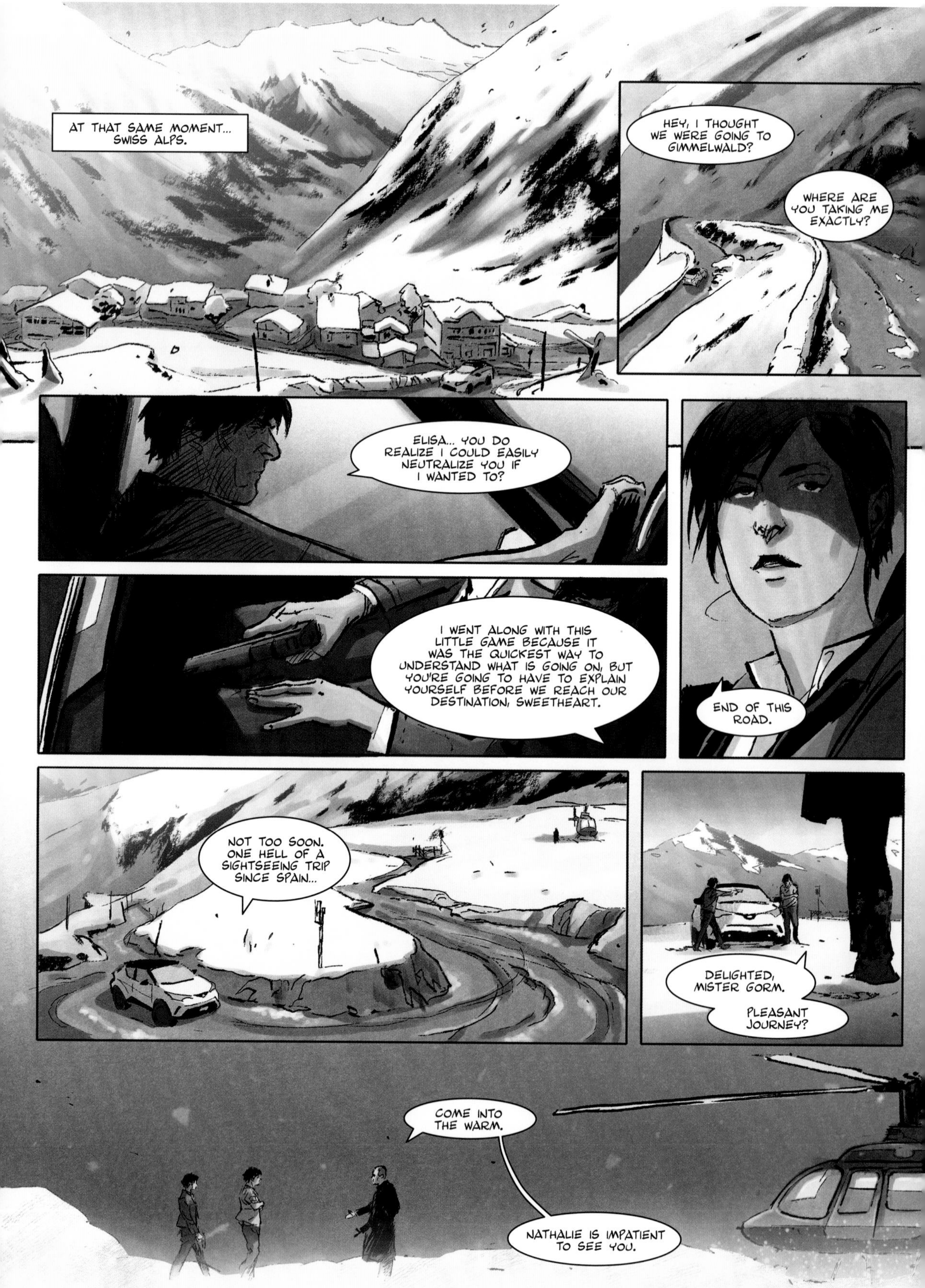
AT THAT SAME MOMENT... SWISS ALPS.
HEY, I THOUGHT WE WERE GOING TO GIMMELWALD?
WHERE ARE YOU TAKING ME EXACTLY?
ELISA... YOU DO REALIZE I COULD EASILY NEUTRALIZE YOU IF I WANTED TO?
I WENT ALONG WITH THIS LITTLE GAME BECAUSE IT WAS THE QUICKEST WAY TO UNDERSTAND WHAT IS GOING ON, BUT YOU'RE GOING TO HAVE TO EXPLAIN YOURSELF BEFORE WE REACH OUR DESTINATION, SWEETHEART.
END OF THIS ROAD.
NOT TOO SOON. ONE HELL OF A SIGHTSEEING TRIP SINCE SPAIN...
DELIGHTED, MISTER GORM.
PLEASANT JOURNEY?
COME INTO THE WARM.
NATHALIE IS IMPATIENT TO SEE YOU.

TO SUMMARISE, YOU HYPNOTIZED ELISA, THEN WAITED FOR THE RIGHT MOMENT TO HAVE HER DRIVE ME OVER TO YOU? SORRY, I MAY BE AMNESIC BUT I'M NOT A MORON.

THAT'S LIKE SOMETHING OUT OF SCIENCE-FICTION.

AND YET YOU UNDERWENT THE SAME TREATMENT NOW SEVENTEEN YEARS AGO.

THE ADLERS WORKED IN MADRID FOR A COMPANY CALLED ABSTERGO, THE PUBLIC FACE FOR THE ORDER OF TEMPLARS.

THE HARD DRIVE THAT YOU STOLE CONTAINS ALL THEIR EXPERIMENTS WITH THE ANIMUS.

THEIR GOAL IS SIMPLE — TO MANIPULATE THE HUMAN BRAIN.

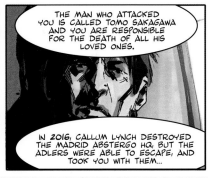

WHEN THE TEMPLARS LAUNCHED THEIR GREAT PURGE IN 2000 TO WIPE OUT THE BROTHERHOOD, THEY USED ASSASSINS LIKE YOU, AGAINST THEIR WILL.

THE MAN WHO ATTACKED YOU IS CALLED TOMO SAKAGAWA AND YOU ARE RESPONSIBLE FOR THE DEATH OF ALL HIS LOVED ONES.

IN 2016, CALLUM LYNCH DESTROYED THE MADRID ABSTERGO HQ, BUT THE ADLERS WERE ABLE TO ESCAPE, AND TOOK YOU WITH THEM...

IT'S A WONDERFUL STORY, MISS CHAPMAN. BUT SINCE I HAD MY MEMORY WIPED, YOU MIGHT AS WELL BE TELLING ME ABOUT SANTA CLAUS.

WHY AM I HERE? WHERE ARE WE GOING?

TO MY HOME.

TO APPEASE YOUR FEARS, IT'S BEST WE LET YOU DISCOVER FOR YOURSELF...

MY PROJECT FOR THE DESTINY OF OUR SPECIES...

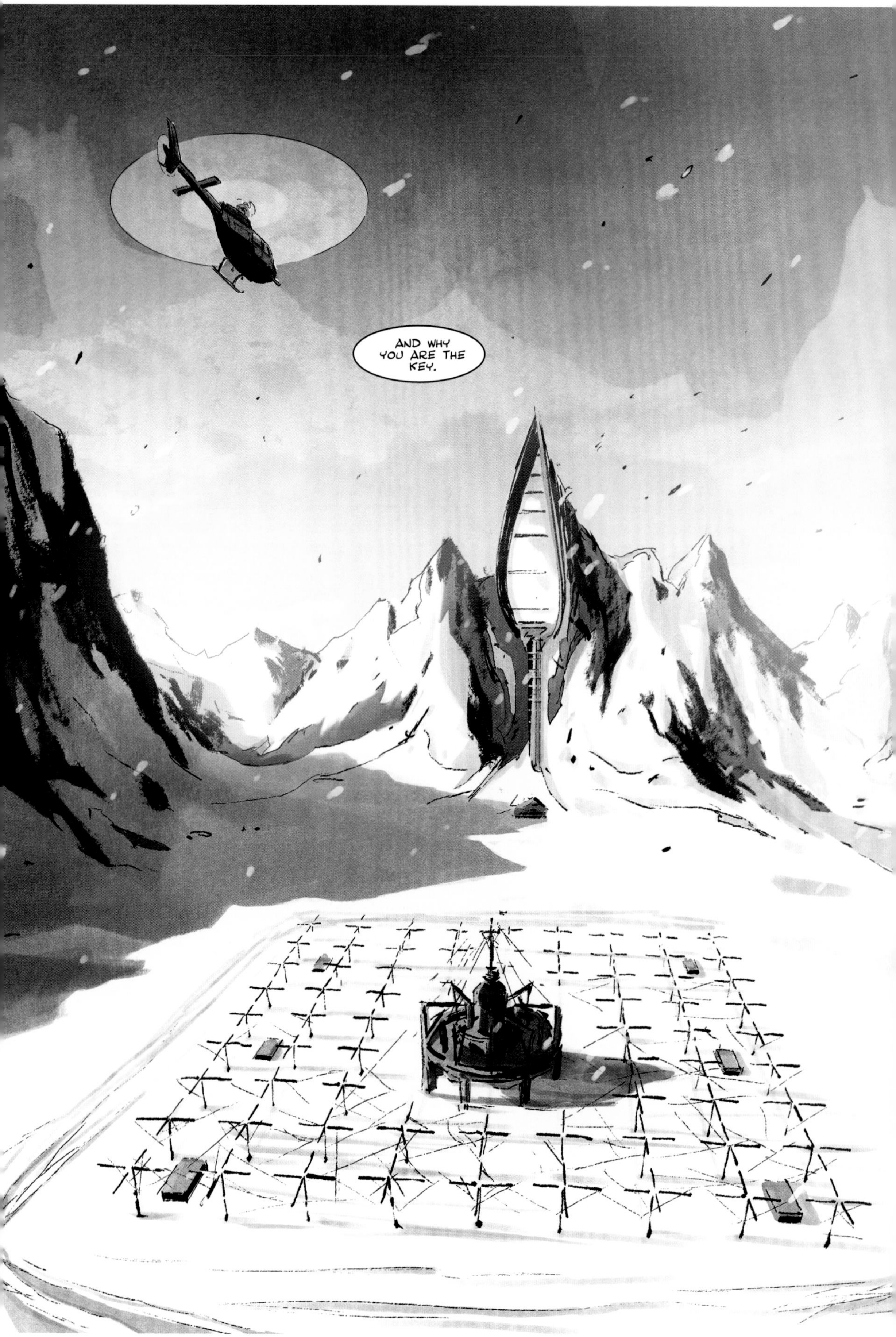
AND WHY YOU ARE THE KEY.

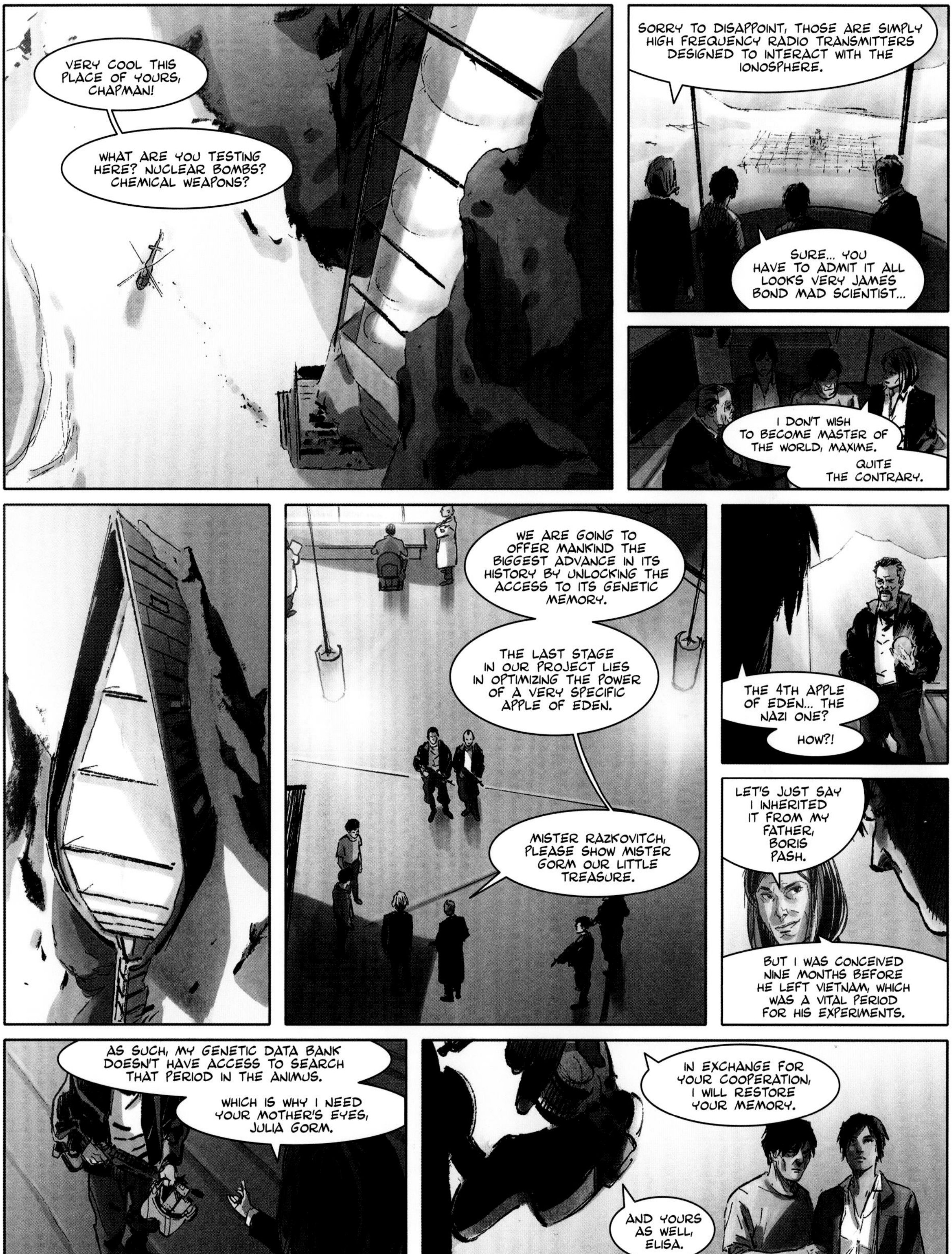
VERY COOL THIS PLACE OF YOURS, CHAPMAN!
WHAT ARE YOU TESTING HERE? NUCLEAR BOMBS? CHEMICAL WEAPONS?
SORRY TO DISAPPOINT, THOSE ARE SIMPLY HIGH FREQUENCY RADIO TRANSMITTERS DESIGNED TO INTERACT WITH THE IONOSPHERE.
SURE... YOU HAVE TO ADMIT IT ALL LOOKS VERY JAMES BOND MAD SCIENTIST...
I DON'T WISH TO BECOME MASTER OF THE WORLD, MAXIME.
QUITE THE CONTRARY.
WE ARE GOING TO OFFER MANKIND THE BIGGEST ADVANCE IN ITS HISTORY BY UNLOCKING THE ACCESS TO ITS GENETIC MEMORY.
THE LAST STAGE IN OUR PROJECT LIES IN OPTIMIZING THE POWER OF A VERY SPECIFIC APPLE OF EDEN.
MISTER RAZKOVITCH, PLEASE SHOW MISTER GORM OUR LITTLE TREASURE.
THE 4TH APPLE OF EDEN... THE NAZI ONE?
HOW?!
LET'S JUST SAY I INHERITED IT FROM MY FATHER, BORIS PASH.
BUT I WAS CONCEIVED NINE MONTHS BEFORE HE LEFT VIETNAM, WHICH WAS A VITAL PERIOD FOR HIS EXPERIMENTS.
AS SUCH, MY GENETIC DATA BANK DOESN'T HAVE ACCESS TO SEARCH THAT PERIOD IN THE ANIMUS.
WHICH IS WHY I NEED YOUR MOTHER'S EYES, JULIA GORM.
IN EXCHANGE FOR YOUR COOPERATION, I WILL RESTORE YOUR MEMORY.
AND YOURS AS WELL, ELISA.

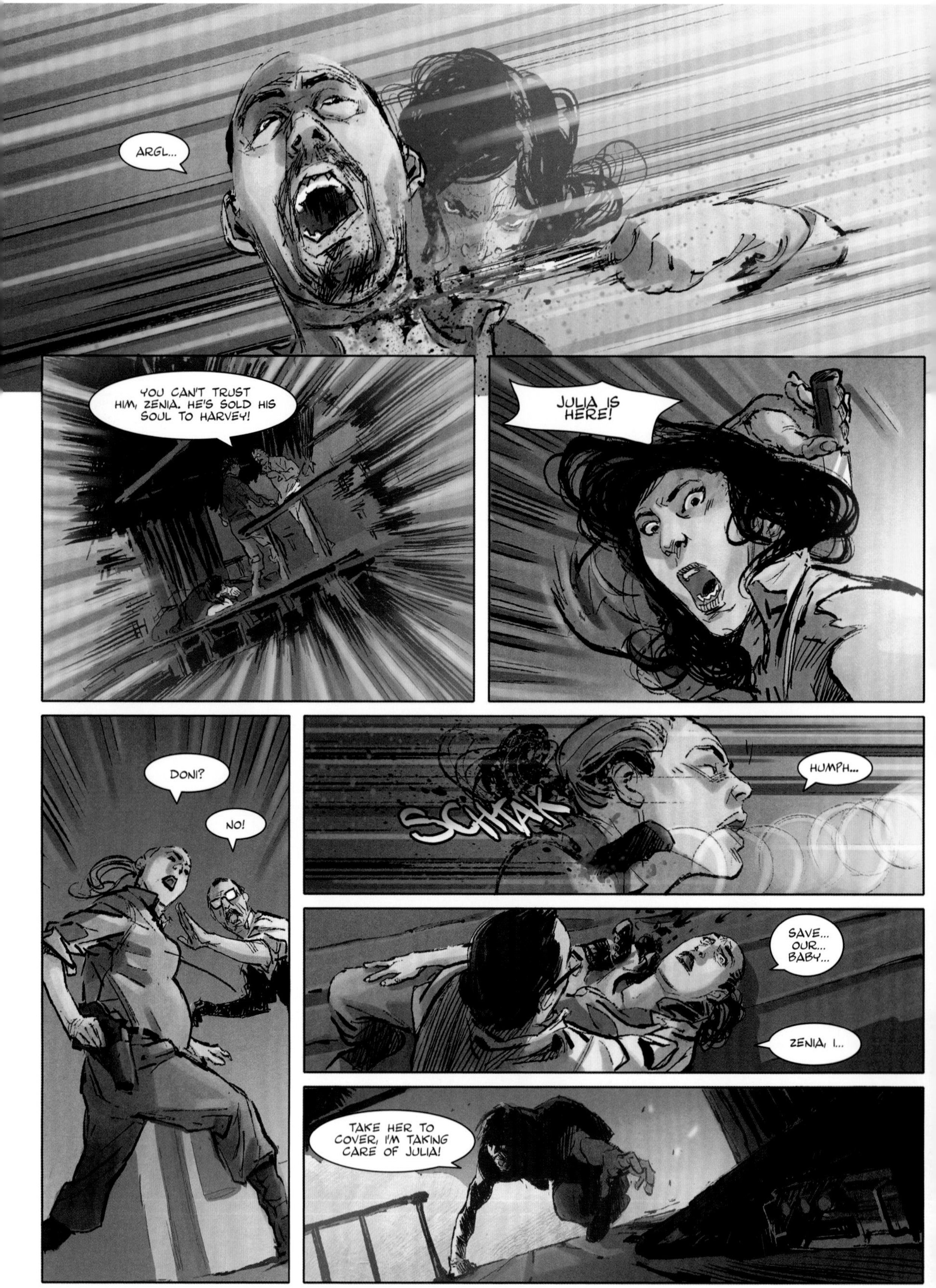
ARGL...
YOU CAN'T TRUST HIM, ZENIA. HE'S SOLD HIS SOUL TO HARVEY!
JULIA IS HERE!
DONI?
NO!
SCHAK
HUMPH...
SAVE... OUR... BABY...
ZENIA, I...
TAKE HER TO COVER, I'M TAKING CARE OF JULIA!

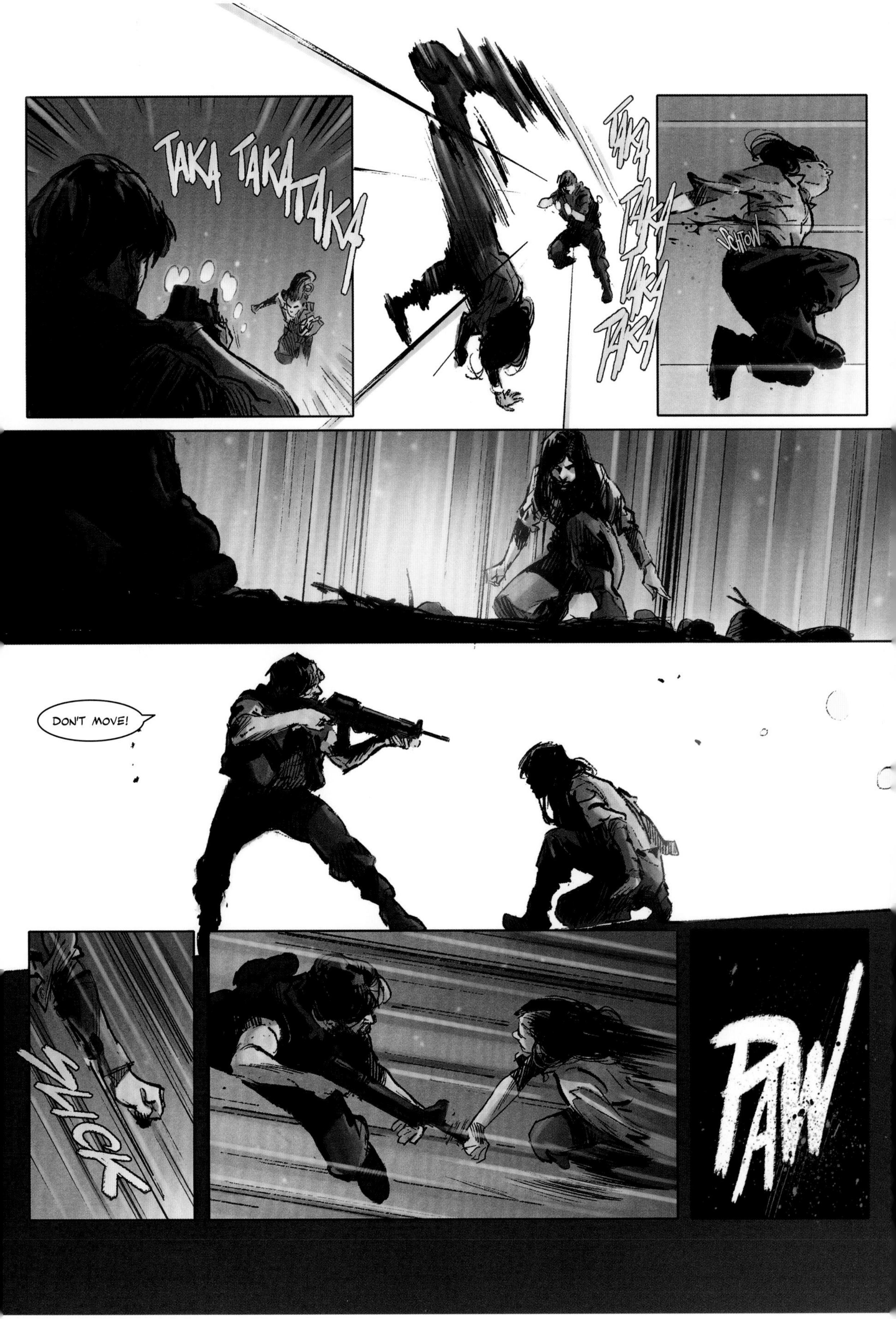
TAKA TAKATAKA
TAKA TAKA TAKA TAKA
SCHTOW
DON'T MOVE!
PAW

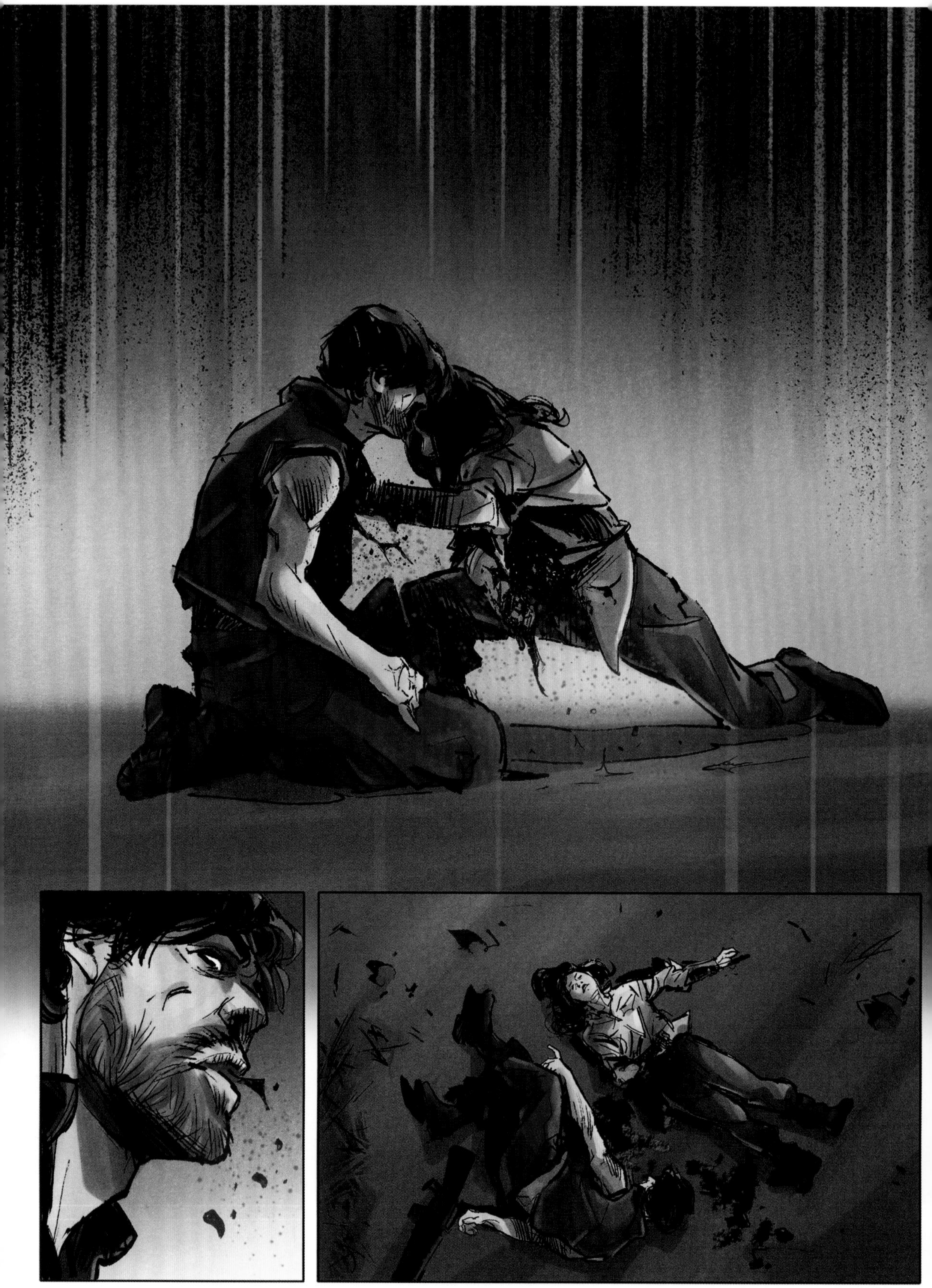

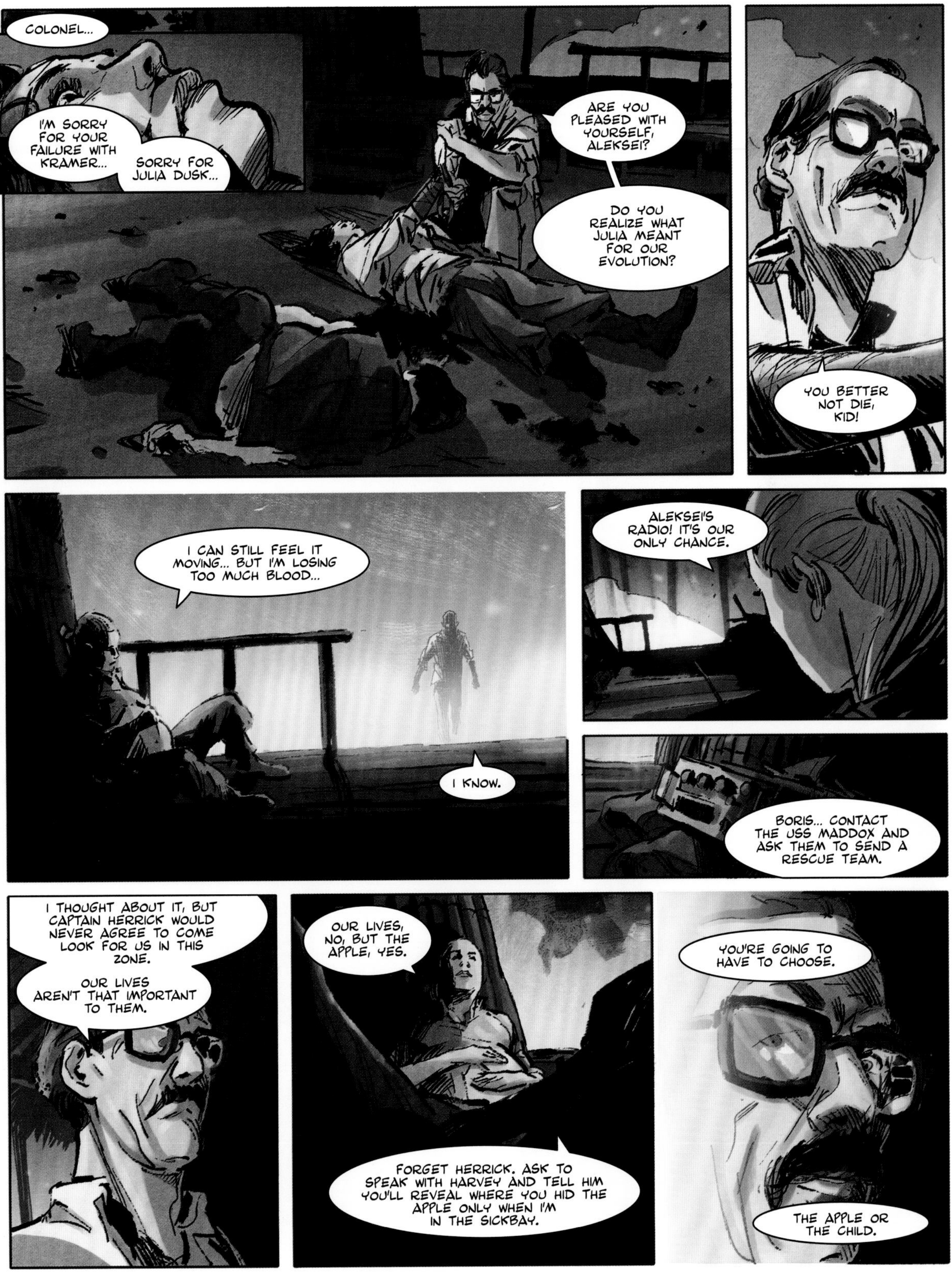
COLONEL...
I'M SORRY FOR YOUR FAILURE WITH KRAMER...
SORRY FOR JULIA DUSK...
ARE YOU PLEASED WITH YOURSELF, ALEKSEI?
DO YOU REALIZE WHAT JULIA MEANT FOR OUR EVOLUTION?
YOU BETTER NOT DIE, KID!
I CAN STILL FEEL IT MOVING... BUT I'M LOSING TOO MUCH BLOOD...
I KNOW.
ALEKSEI'S RADIO! IT'S OUR ONLY CHANCE.
BORIS... CONTACT THE USS MADDOX AND ASK THEM TO SEND A RESCUE TEAM.
I THOUGHT ABOUT IT, BUT CAPTAIN HERRICK WOULD NEVER AGREE TO COME LOOK FOR US IN THIS ZONE.
OUR LIVES AREN'T THAT IMPORTANT TO THEM.
OUR LIVES, NO, BUT THE APPLE, YES.
FORGET HERRICK. ASK TO SPEAK WITH HARVEY AND TELL HIM YOU'LL REVEAL WHERE YOU HID THE APPLE ONLY WHEN I'M IN THE SICKBAY.
YOU'RE GOING TO HAVE TO CHOOSE.
THE APPLE OR THE CHILD.

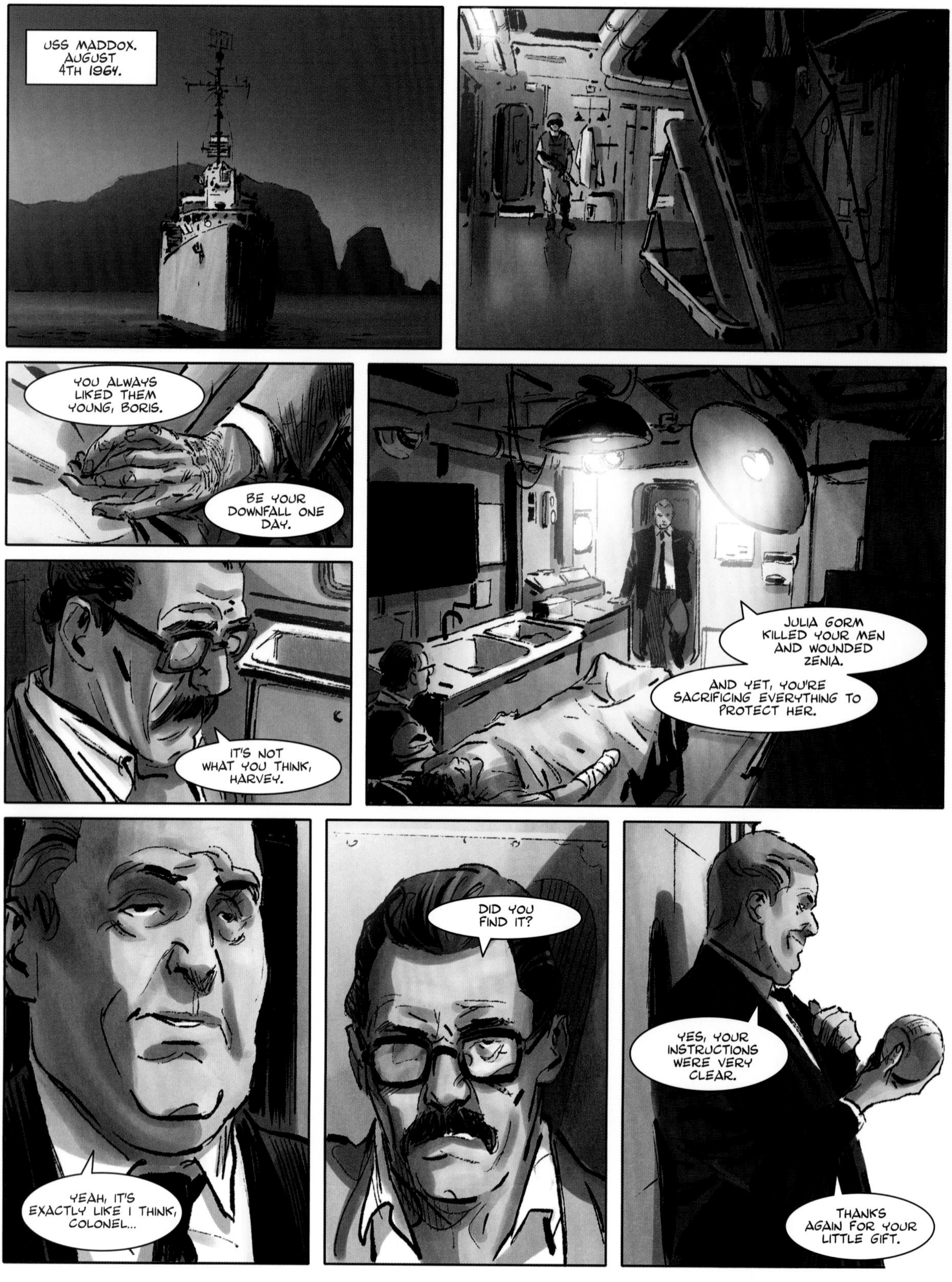
USS MADDOX. AUGUST 4TH 1964.
YOU ALWAYS LIKED THEM YOUNG, BORIS.
BE YOUR DOWNFALL ONE DAY.
JULIA GORM KILLED YOUR MEN AND WOUNDED ZENIA.
AND YET, YOU'RE SACRIFICING EVERYTHING TO PROTECT HER.
IT'S NOT WHAT YOU THINK, HARVEY.
YEAH, IT'S EXACTLY LIKE I THINK, COLONEL...
DID YOU FIND IT?
YES, YOUR INSTRUCTIONS WERE VERY CLEAR.
THANKS AGAIN FOR YOUR LITTLE GIFT.

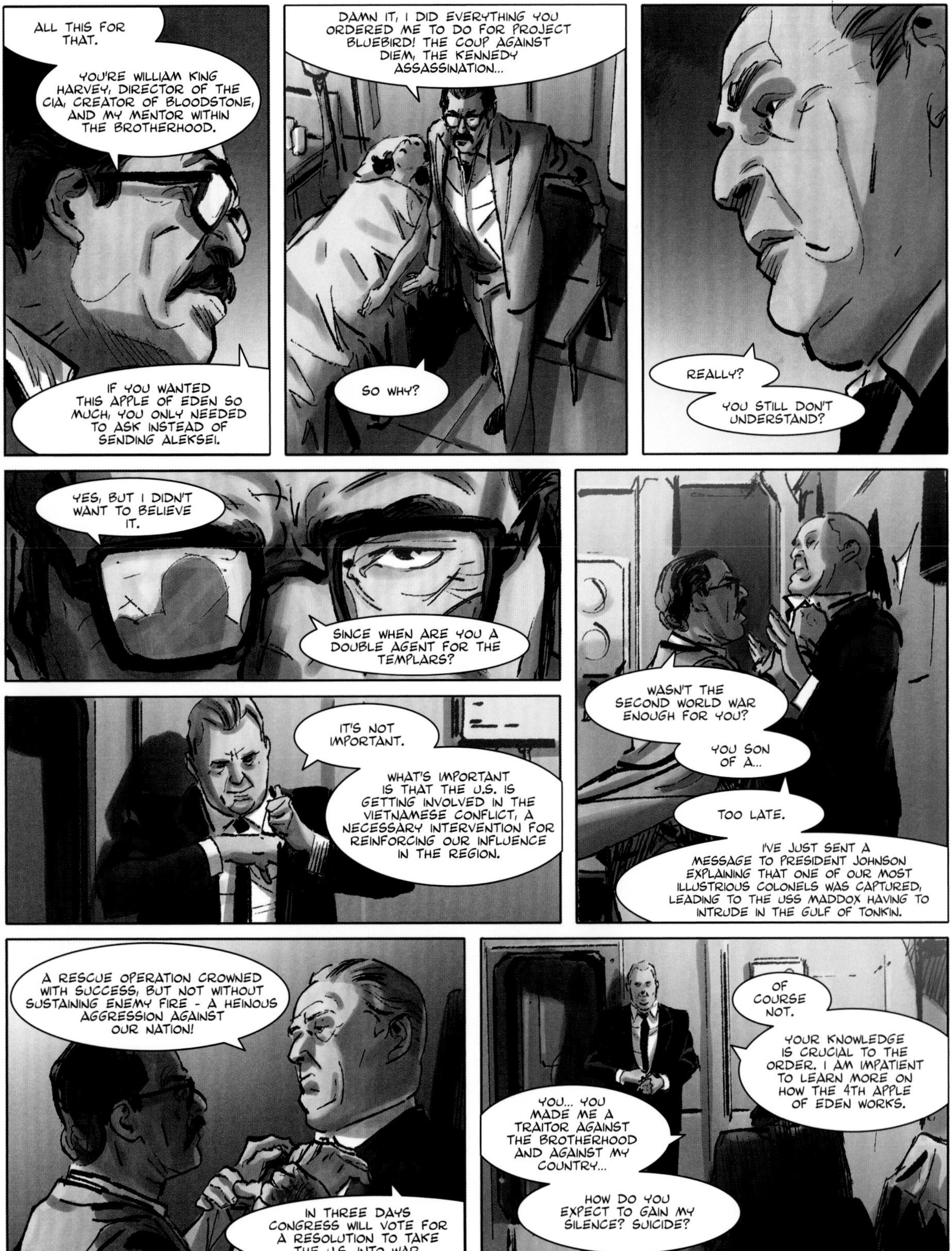
ALL THIS FOR THAT.
YOU'RE WILLIAM KING HARVEY, DIRECTOR OF THE CIA, CREATOR OF BLOODSTONE, AND MY MENTOR WITHIN THE BROTHERHOOD.
IF YOU WANTED THIS APPLE OF EDEN SO MUCH, YOU ONLY NEEDED TO ASK INSTEAD OF SENDING ALEKSEI.
DAMN IT, I DID EVERYTHING YOU ORDERED ME TO DO FOR PROJECT BLUEBIRD! THE COUP AGAINST DIEM, THE KENNEDY ASSASSINATION...
SO WHY?
REALLY?
YOU STILL DON'T UNDERSTAND?
YES, BUT I DIDN'T WANT TO BELIEVE IT.
SINCE WHEN ARE YOU A DOUBLE AGENT FOR THE TEMPLARS?
IT'S NOT IMPORTANT.
WHAT'S IMPORTANT IS THAT THE U.S. IS GETTING INVOLVED IN THE VIETNAMESE CONFLICT, A NECESSARY INTERVENTION FOR REINFORCING OUR INFLUENCE IN THE REGION.
WASN'T THE SECOND WORLD WAR ENOUGH FOR YOU?
YOU SON OF A...
TOO LATE.
I'VE JUST SENT A MESSAGE TO PRESIDENT JOHNSON EXPLAINING THAT ONE OF OUR MOST ILLUSTRIOUS COLONELS WAS CAPTURED, LEADING TO THE USS MADDOX HAVING TO INTRUDE IN THE GULF OF TONKIN.
A RESCUE OPERATION CROWNED WITH SUCCESS, BUT NOT WITHOUT SUSTAINING ENEMY FIRE - A HEINOUS AGGRESSION AGAINST OUR NATION!
IN THREE DAYS CONGRESS WILL VOTE FOR A RESOLUTION TO TAKE THE U.S. INTO WAR.
YOU... YOU MADE ME A TRAITOR AGAINST THE BROTHERHOOD AND AGAINST MY COUNTRY...
HOW DO YOU EXPECT TO GAIN MY SILENCE? SUICIDE?
OF COURSE NOT.
YOUR KNOWLEDGE IS CRUCIAL TO THE ORDER. I AM IMPATIENT TO LEARN MORE ON HOW THE 4TH APPLE OF EDEN WORKS.

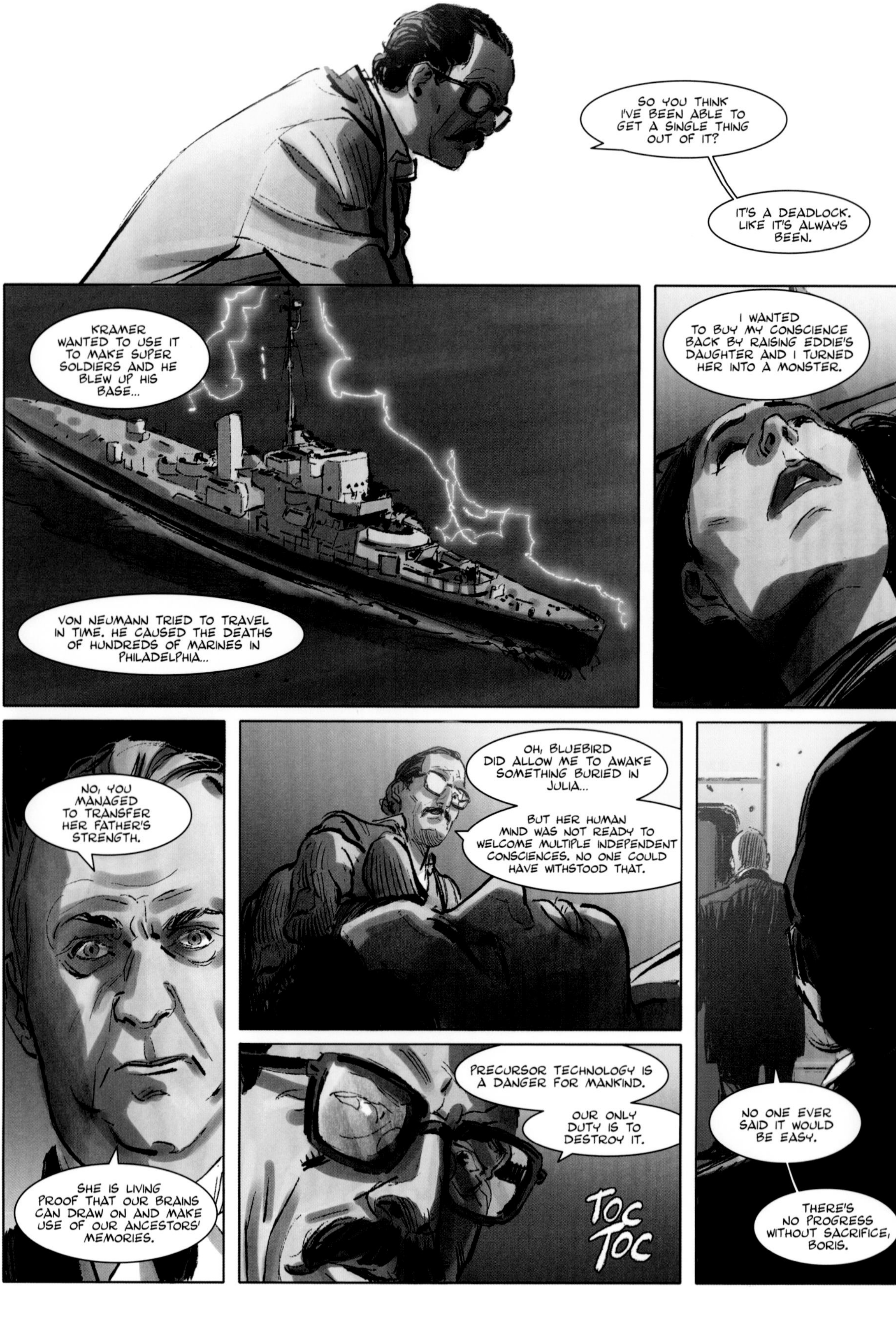

SO YOU THINK I'VE BEEN ABLE TO GET A SINGLE THING OUT OF IT?
IT'S A DEADLOCK. LIKE IT'S ALWAYS BEEN.
KRAMER WANTED TO USE IT TO MAKE SUPER SOLDIERS AND HE BLEW UP HIS BASE...
VON NEUMANN TRIED TO TRAVEL IN TIME. HE CAUSED THE DEATHS OF HUNDREDS OF MARINES IN PHILADELPHIA...
I WANTED TO BUY MY CONSCIENCE BACK BY RAISING EDDIE'S DAUGHTER AND I TURNED HER INTO A MONSTER.
NO, YOU MANAGED TO TRANSFER HER FATHER'S STRENGTH.
SHE IS LIVING PROOF THAT OUR BRAINS CAN DRAW ON AND MAKE USE OF OUR ANCESTORS' MEMORIES.
OH, BLUEBIRD DID ALLOW ME TO AWAKE SOMETHING BURIED IN JULIA...
BUT HER HUMAN MIND WAS NOT READY TO WELCOME MULTIPLE INDEPENDENT CONSCIENCES. NO ONE COULD HAVE WITHSTOOD THAT.
PRECURSOR TECHNOLOGY IS A DANGER FOR MANKIND.
OUR ONLY DUTY IS TO DESTROY IT.
TOC TOC
NO ONE EVER SAID IT WOULD BE EASY.
THERE'S NO PROGRESS WITHOUT SACRIFICE, BORIS.

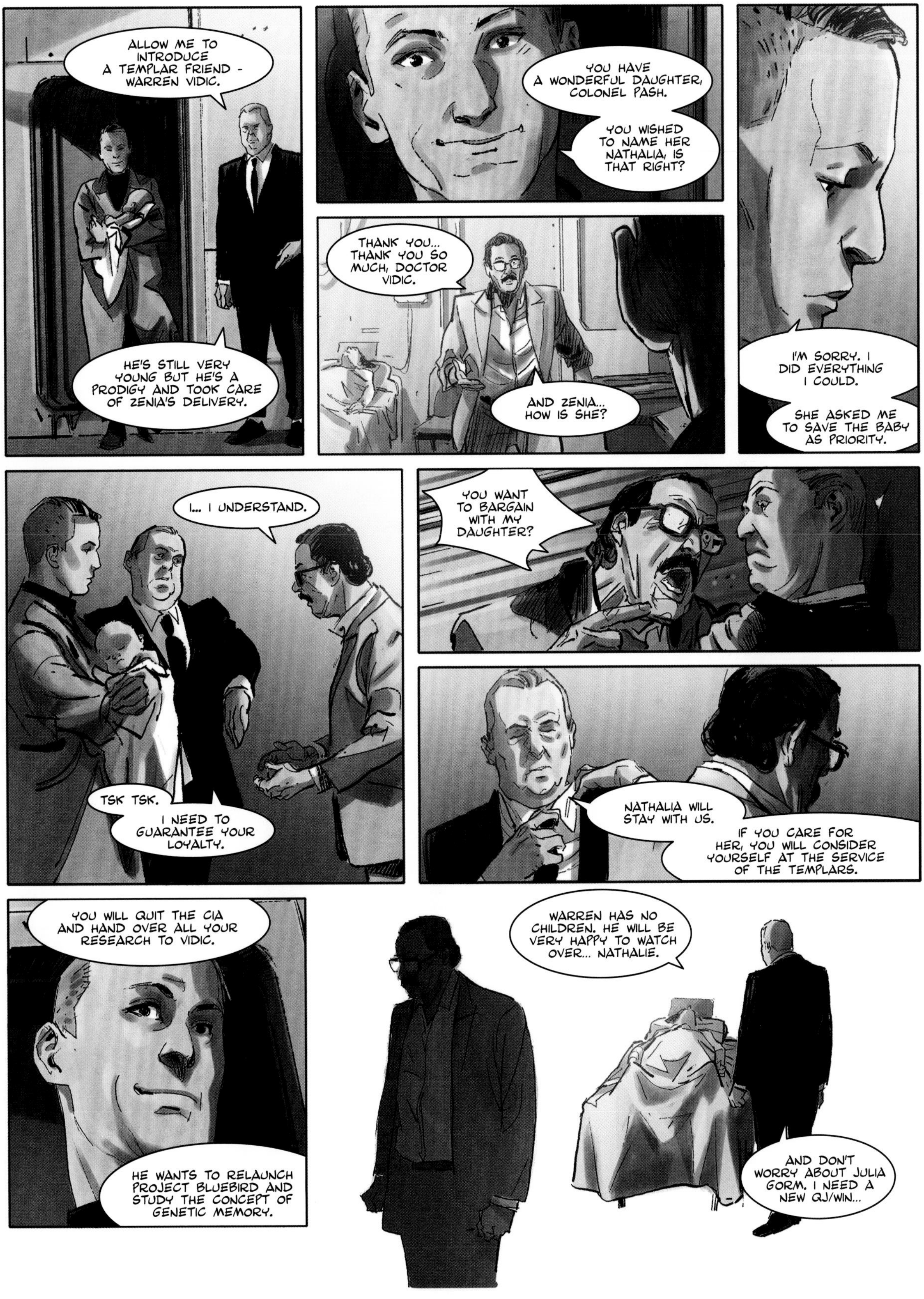
ALLOW ME TO INTRODUCE A TEMPLAR FRIEND - WARREN VIDIC.
HE'S STILL VERY YOUNG BUT HE'S A PRODIGY AND TOOK CARE OF ZENIA'S DELIVERY.
YOU HAVE A WONDERFUL DAUGHTER, COLONEL PASH.
YOU WISHED TO NAME HER NATHALIA, IS THAT RIGHT?
THANK YOU... THANK YOU SO MUCH, DOCTOR VIDIC.
AND ZENIA... HOW IS SHE?
I'M SORRY. I DID EVERYTHING I COULD.
SHE ASKED ME TO SAVE THE BABY AS PRIORITY.
I... I UNDERSTAND.
TSK TSK.
I NEED TO GUARANTEE YOUR LOYALTY.
YOU WANT TO BARGAIN WITH MY DAUGHTER?
NATHALIA WILL STAY WITH US.
IF YOU CARE FOR HER, YOU WILL CONSIDER YOURSELF AT THE SERVICE OF THE TEMPLARS.
YOU WILL QUIT THE CIA AND HAND OVER ALL YOUR RESEARCH TO VIDIC.
HE WANTS TO RELAUNCH PROJECT BLUEBIRD AND STUDY THE CONCEPT OF GENETIC MEMORY.
WARREN HAS NO CHILDREN. HE WILL BE VERY HAPPY TO WATCH OVER... NATHALIE.
AND DON'T WORRY ABOUT JULIA GORM. I NEED A NEW QJ/WIN...

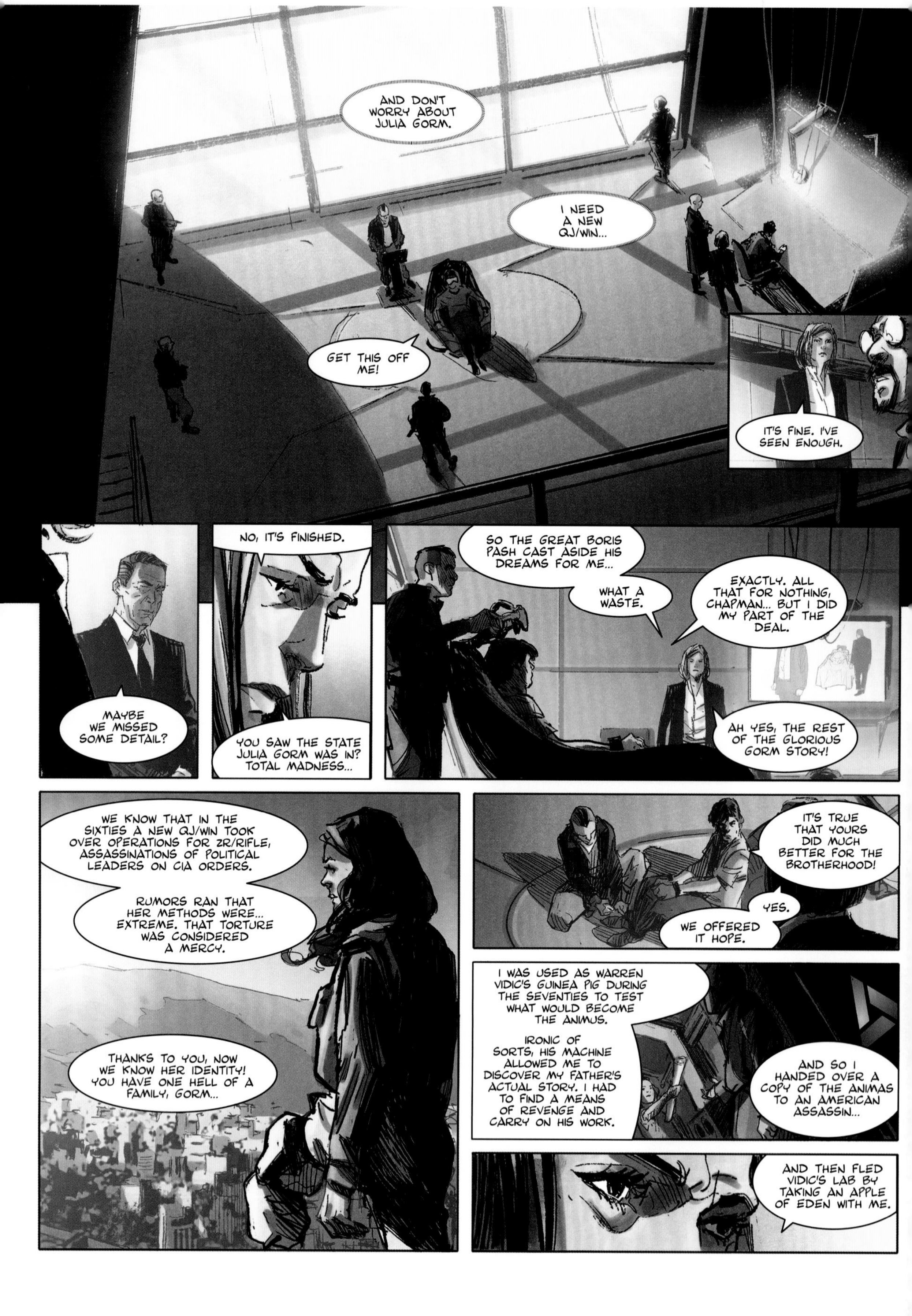
AND DON'T WORRY ABOUT JULIA GORM.
I NEED A NEW QJ/WIN...
GET THIS OFF ME!
IT'S FINE. I'VE SEEN ENOUGH.
MAYBE WE MISSED SOME DETAIL?
NO, IT'S FINISHED.
YOU SAW THE STATE JULIA GORM WAS IN? TOTAL MADNESS...
SO THE GREAT BORIS PASH CAST ASIDE HIS DREAMS FOR ME...
WHAT A WASTE.
EXACTLY. ALL THAT FOR NOTHING, CHAPMAN... BUT I DID MY PART OF THE DEAL.
AH YES, THE REST OF THE GLORIOUS GORM STORY!
WE KNOW THAT IN THE SIXTIES A NEW QJ/WIN TOOK OVER OPERATIONS FOR ZR/RIFLE, ASSASSINATIONS OF POLITICAL LEADERS ON CIA ORDERS.
RUMORS RAN THAT HER METHODS WERE... EXTREME. THAT TORTURE WAS CONSIDERED A MERCY.
THANKS TO YOU, NOW WE KNOW HER IDENTITY! YOU HAVE ONE HELL OF A FAMILY, GORM...
IT'S TRUE THAT YOURS DID MUCH BETTER FOR THE BROTHERHOOD!
YES.
WE OFFERED IT HOPE.
I WAS USED AS WARREN VIDIC'S GUINEA PIG DURING THE SEVENTIES TO TEST WHAT WOULD BECOME THE ANIMUS.
IRONIC OF SORTS, HIS MACHINE ALLOWED ME TO DISCOVER MY FATHER'S ACTUAL STORY. I HAD TO FIND A MEANS OF REVENGE AND CARRY ON HIS WORK.
AND SO I HANDED OVER A COPY OF THE ANIMAS TO AN AMERICAN ASSASSIN...
AND THEN FLED VIDIC'S LAB BY TAKING AN APPLE OF EDEN WITH ME.

THAT'S A MOVING STORY, CHAPMAN.

IT WOULDN'T TAKE MUCH FOR ME TO FEEL BAD IF I COULDN'T GIVE IT A HAPPY ENDING.

ON THE CONTRARY, WE NOW HAVE PROOF THAT YOUR MOTHER LIVED WITH THE MEMORY OF EDDIE GORM FOR SOME TIME.

THAT WILL DO.

ACTIVATE ALL OUR PHASED ANTENNAS. WE'RE STARTING.

NATHALIE, WE STILL HAVEN'T LEARNED HOW TO CONTROL THE APPLE OF EDEN.

WE NEED TO CANCEL.

I AM NOT MY FATHER, STANISLAS.

THERE'S NO QUESTION OF ATTEMPTING A COMPLETE MEMORY RESURRECTION LIKE WITH JULIA.

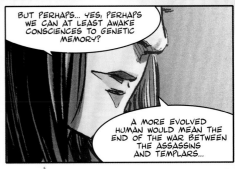

BUT PERHAPS... YES, PERHAPS WE CAN AT LEAST AWAKE CONSCIENCES TO GENETIC MEMORY?

A MORE EVOLVED HUMAN WOULD MEAN THE END OF THE WAR BETWEEN THE ASSASSINS AND TEMPLARS...

SET THE APPLE TO 5% OF ITS POWER.

UNDERSTOOD.

AND AIM BLUEBIRD SOLELY ON GIMMELWALD FOR NOW.

COUNTDOWN ONE HOUR BEFORE RELEASING THE RADIO FREQUENCIES INTO THE IONOSPHERE.

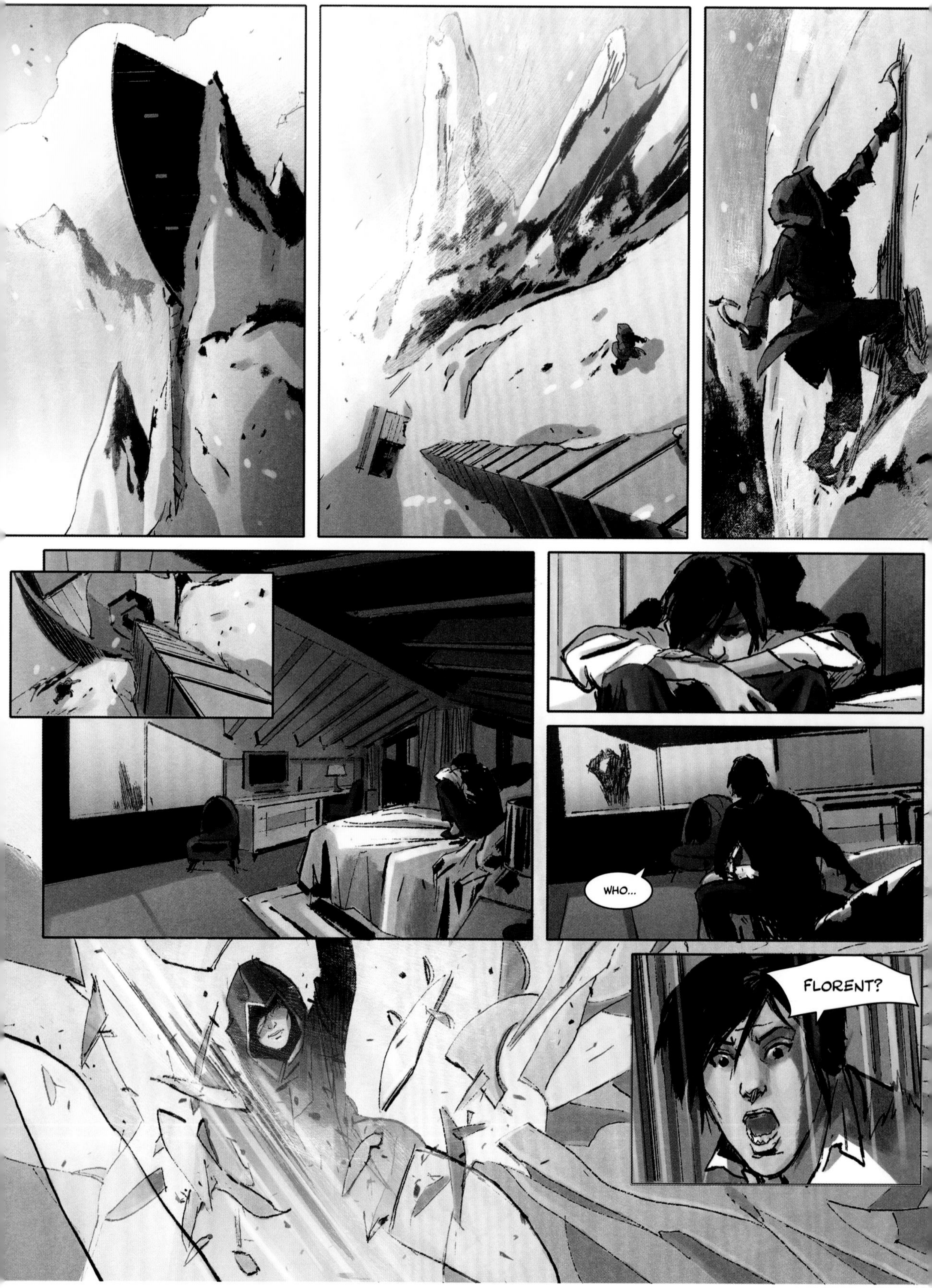
WHO...
FLORENT?

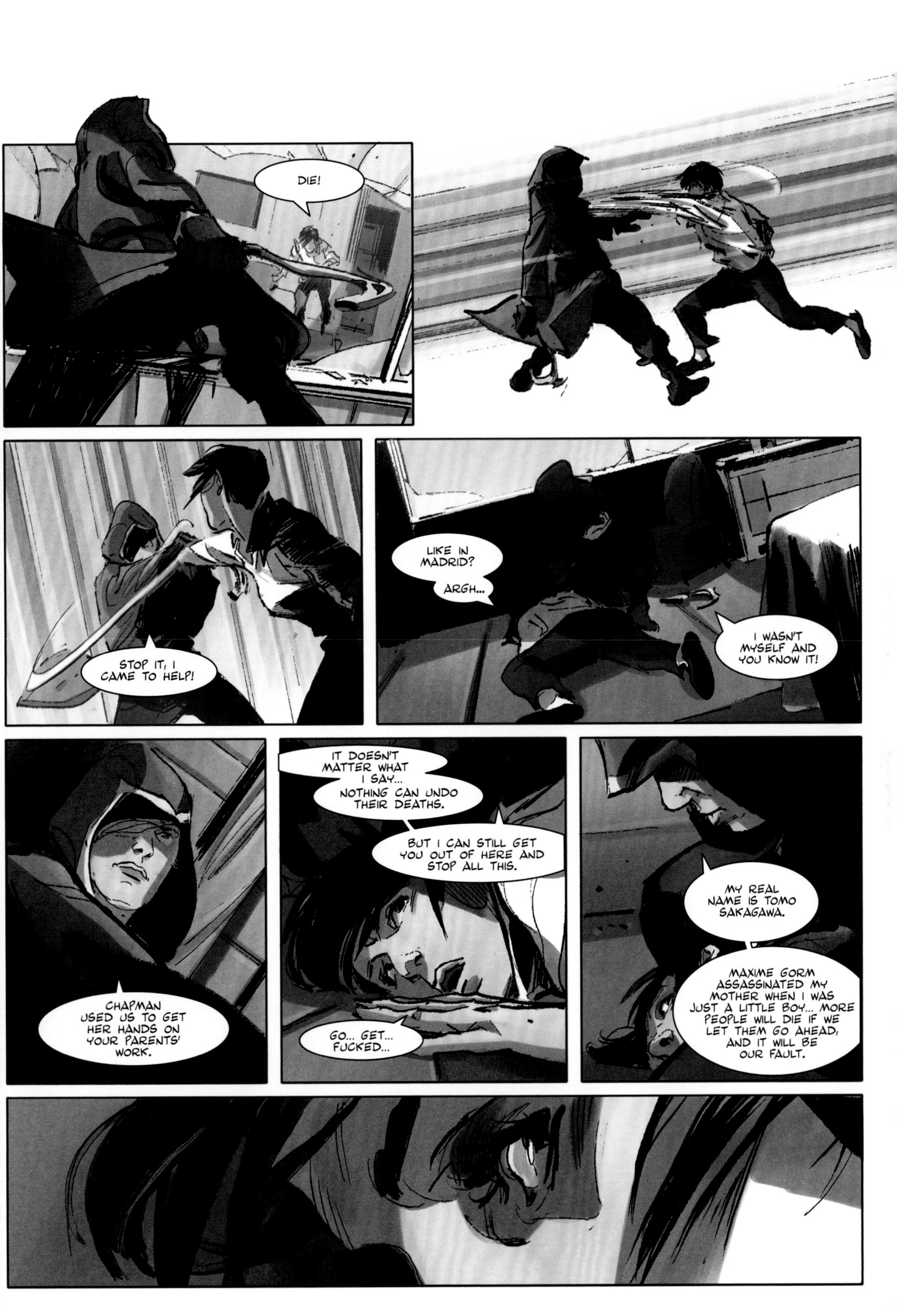
DIE!
STOP IT, I CAME TO HELP!
LIKE IN MADRID?
ARGH...
I WASN'T MYSELF AND YOU KNOW IT!
CHAPMAN USED US TO GET HER HANDS ON YOUR PARENTS' WORK.
IT DOESN'T MATTER WHAT I SAY...
NOTHING CAN UNDO THEIR DEATHS.
BUT I CAN STILL GET YOU OUT OF HERE AND STOP ALL THIS.
GO... GET... FUCKED...
MY REAL NAME IS TOMO SAKAGAWA.
MAXIME GORM ASSASSINATED MY MOTHER WHEN I WAS JUST A LITTLE BOY... MORE PEOPLE WILL DIE IF WE LET THEM GO AHEAD, AND IT WILL BE OUR FAULT.

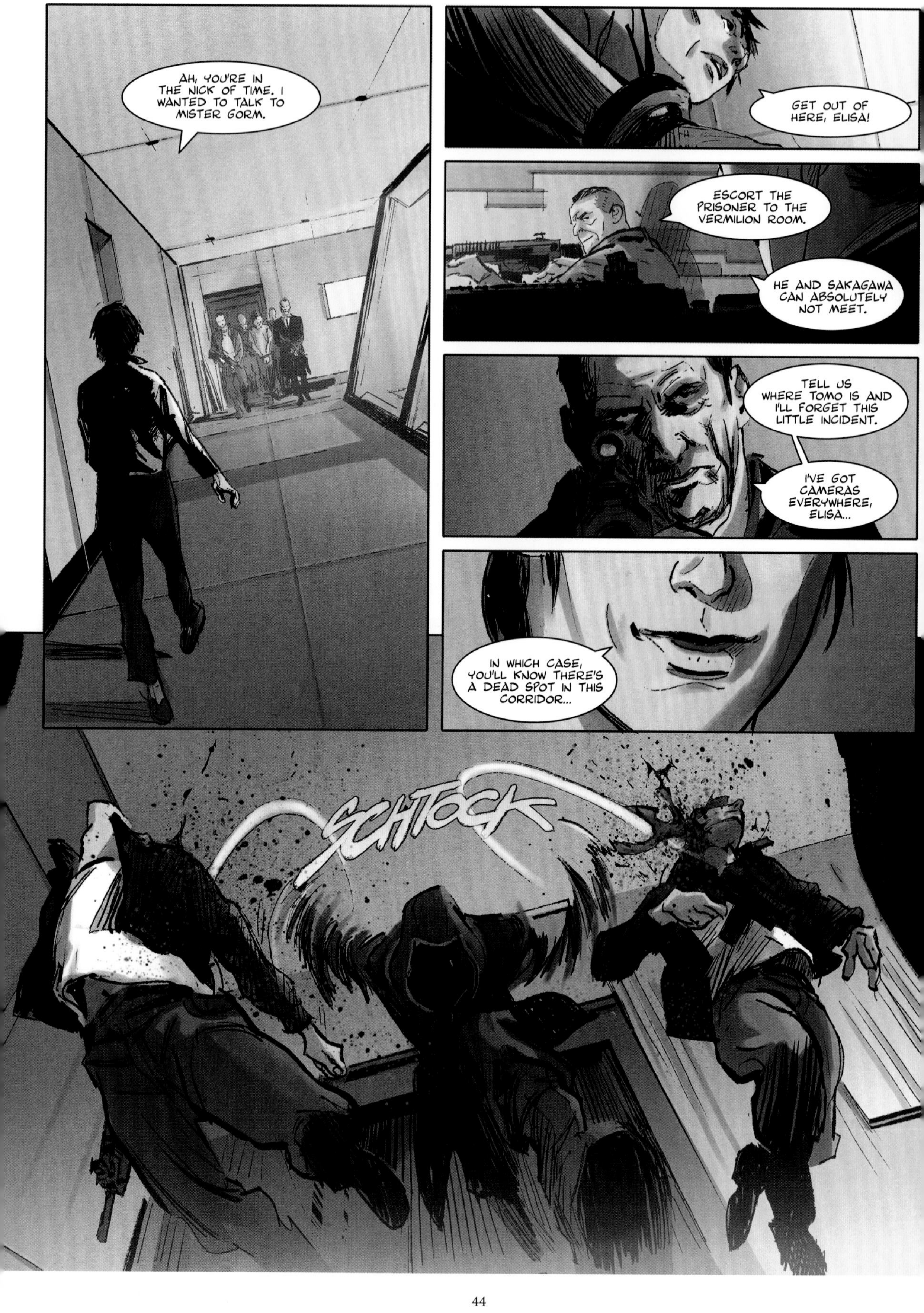
AH, YOU'RE IN THE NICK OF TIME. I WANTED TO TALK TO MISTER GORM.
GET OUT OF HERE, ELISA!
ESCORT THE PRISONER TO THE VERMILION ROOM.
HE AND SAKAGAWA CAN ABSOLUTELY NOT MEET.
TELL US WHERE TOMO IS AND I'LL FORGET THIS LITTLE INCIDENT.
I'VE GOT CAMERAS EVERYWHERE, ELISA...
IN WHICH CASE, YOU'LL KNOW THERE'S A DEAD SPOT IN THIS CORRIDOR...
SCHTOCK

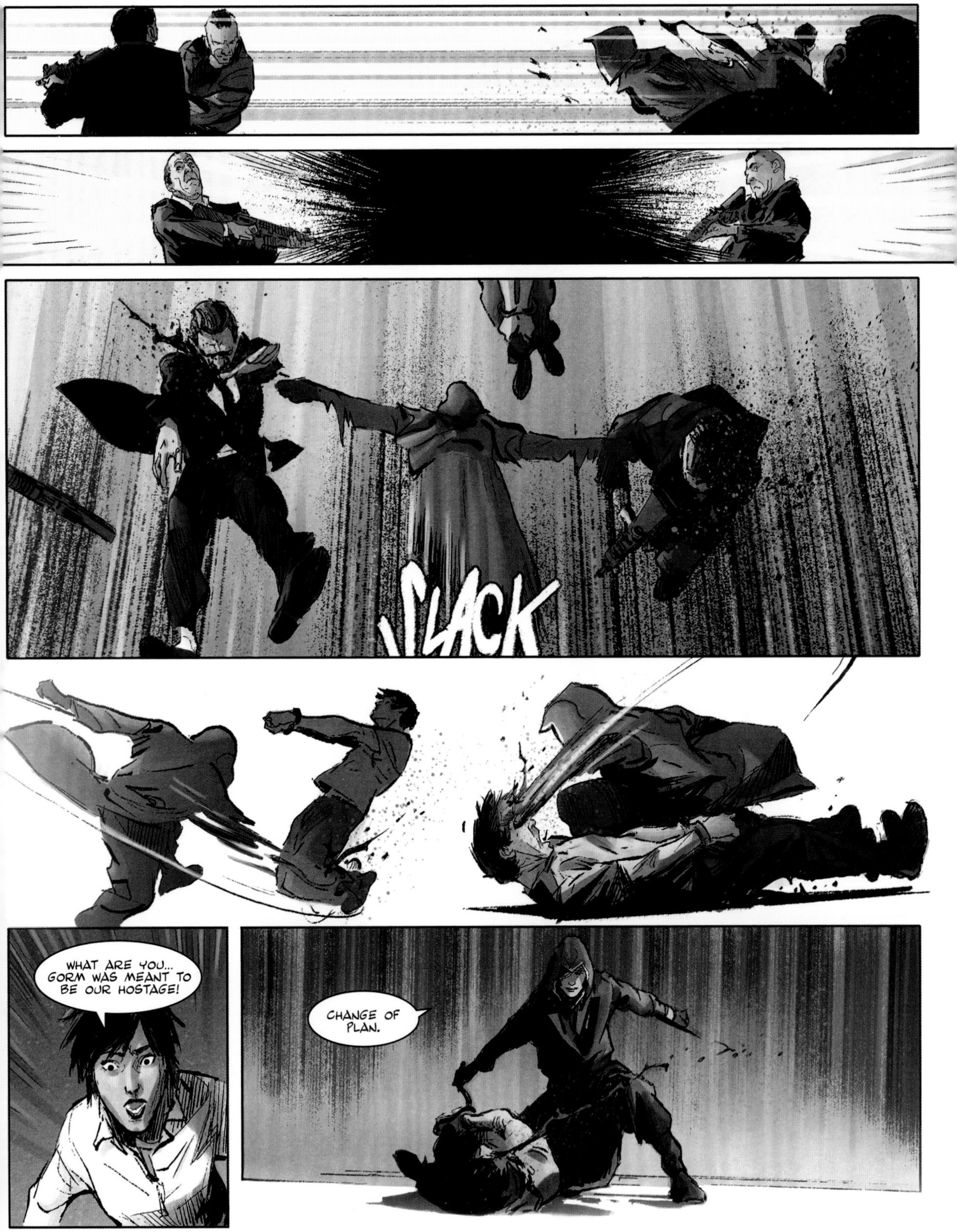
SLACK
WHAT ARE YOU... GORM WAS MEANT TO BE OUR HOSTAGE!
CHANGE OF PLAN.

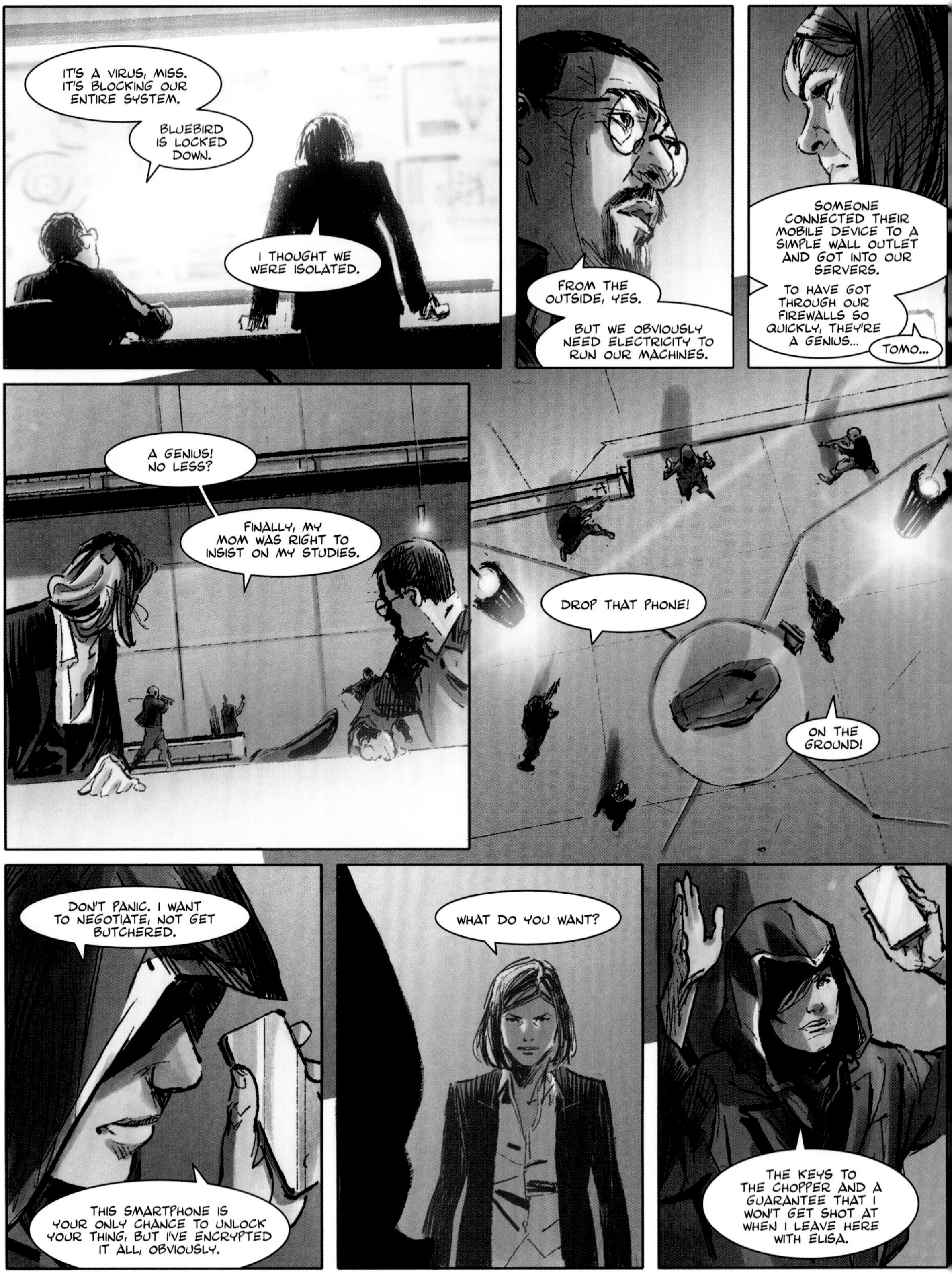
IT'S A VIRUS, MISS. IT'S BLOCKING OUR ENTIRE SYSTEM.
BLUEBIRD IS LOCKED DOWN.
I THOUGHT WE WERE ISOLATED.
FROM THE OUTSIDE, YES.
BUT WE OBVIOUSLY NEED ELECTRICITY TO RUN OUR MACHINES.
SOMEONE CONNECTED THEIR MOBILE DEVICE TO A SIMPLE WALL OUTLET AND GOT INTO OUR SERVERS.
TO HAVE GOT THROUGH OUR FIREWALLS SO QUICKLY, THEY'RE A GENIUS...
TOMO...
A GENIUS! NO LESS?
FINALLY, MY MOM WAS RIGHT TO INSIST ON MY STUDIES.
DROP THAT PHONE!
ON THE GROUND!
DON'T PANIC. I WANT TO NEGOTIATE, NOT GET BUTCHERED.
THIS SMARTPHONE IS YOUR ONLY CHANCE TO UNLOCK YOUR THING, BUT I'VE ENCRYPTED IT ALL, OBVIOUSLY.
WHAT DO YOU WANT?
THE KEYS TO THE CHOPPER AND A GUARANTEE THAT I WON'T GET SHOT AT WHEN I LEAVE HERE WITH ELISA.

HOW NAÏVE DO I LOOK?

NATHALIE.

I DON'T BELIEVE THAT YOUR BIG PROJECT HAS A HOPE OF LEAVING THE GROUND.

MY ONLY PRIORITY IS ELISA'S AND MY SURVIVAL.

GIVE ME ANY OLD PHONE IN EXCHANGE FOR THIS ONE AND I'LL REMOTELY UNLOCK MINE WHEN I'M SAFE.

ACCOMPANY TOMO AND ELISA TO THE HELICOPTER AND GIVE THEM YOUR PHONE.

THINK.

BY OFFERING GENETIC MEMORY TO THE ENTIRE POPULATION, BLUEBIRD WILL BRING UNIVERSAL WISDOM AND GUIDE US TO TRUE FREEDOM.

BEING SADDLED WITH THE MEMORIES OF OUR ANCESTORS ISN'T FREEDOM, CHAPMAN..

QUITE THE OPPOSITE, IT'S HAVING THE CHOICE TO MAKE DECISIONS FREE OF INFLUENCE.

IN THAT CASE, RENDEZVOUS IN THE NEW WORLD, TOMO.

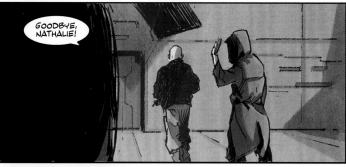

GOODBYE, NATHALIE!

YOU'RE LETTING HIM ESCAPE?

ELISA ADLER IS STILL UNDER MY HYPNOTIC INFLUENCE.

ONCE BLUEBIRD RELAUNCHES, I WILL ASK HER TO BRING TOMO BACK HERE.

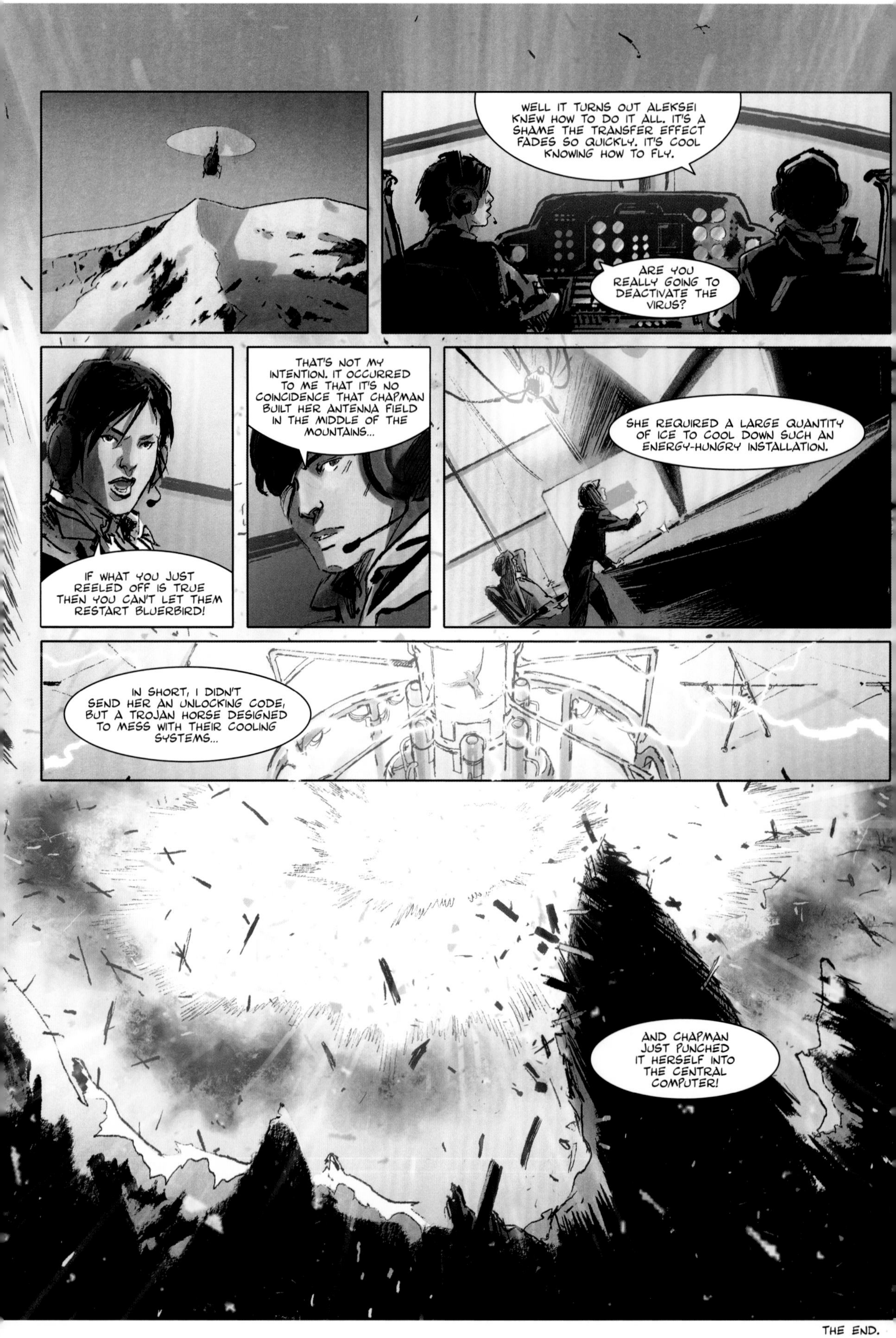
WELL IT TURNS OUT ALEKSEI KNEW HOW TO DO IT ALL. IT'S A SHAME THE TRANSFER EFFECT FADES SO QUICKLY. IT'S COOL KNOWING HOW TO FLY.
ARE YOU REALLY GOING TO DEACTIVATE THE VIRUS?
IF WHAT YOU JUST REELED OFF IS TRUE THEN YOU CAN'T LET THEM RESTART BLUERBIRD!
THAT'S NOT MY INTENTION. IT OCCURRED TO ME THAT IT'S NO COINCIDENCE THAT CHAPMAN BUILT HER ANTENNA FIELD IN THE MIDDLE OF THE MOUNTAINS...
SHE REQUIRED A LARGE QUANTITY OF ICE TO COOL DOWN SUCH AN ENERGY-HUNGRY INSTALLATION.
IN SHORT, I DIDN'T SEND HER AN UNLOCKING CODE, BUT A TROJAN HORSE DESIGNED TO MESS WITH THEIR COOLING SYSTEMS...
AND CHAPMAN JUST PUNCHED IT HERSELF INTO THE CENTRAL COMPUTER!

THE END.